Legends a from Mediæval Literature

Martha Hale Shackford

Alpha Editions

This edition published in 2022

ISBN : 9789356716131

Design and Setting By
Alpha Editions
www.alphaedis.com
Email - info@alphaedis.com

As per information held with us this book is in Public Domain.
This book is a reproduction of an important historical work. Alpha Editions uses the best technology to reproduce historical work in the same manner it was first published to preserve its original nature. Any marks or number seen are left intentionally to preserve its true form.

Contents

PREFACE .... - 1 -

INTRODUCTION .... - 2 -

PROEM .... - 5 -

    OF MAN'S BODY[3] .... - 5 -

    OF MAN'S SOUL .... - 5 -

DEBATE .... - 7 -

    THE AMOROUS CONTENTION OF
    PHILLIS AND FLORA[4] .... - 7 -

    THE PLEADING OF THE ROSE AND
    OF THE VIOLET[25] .... - 22 -

VISION .... - 27 -

    THE PURGATORY OF SAINT
    PATRICK[26] .... - 27 -

SAINTS' LIVES .... - 37 -

    THE LIFE OF SAINT BRANDON[31] .... - 37 -

    THE LIFE OF SAINT
    MARGARET[39] .... - 48 -

PIOUS TALES .... - 52 -

A MIRACLE OF GOD'S BODY[40] .... - 52 -

A MIRACLE OF THE VIRGIN[41] .... - 53 -

THE TRANSLATION OF SAINT
THOMAS OF CANTERBURY[42] .... - 55 -

ALLEGORY .... - 59 -

AN EXTRACT FROM "THE CASTLE
OF LOVE"[43] .... - 59 -

BESTIARY .... - 61 -

THE LION[45] .... - 61 -

THE EAGLE .... - 62 -

THE WHALE .... - 62 -

THE SIREN .... - 63 -

LAPIDARY .... - 65 -

EXTRACTS FROM LAPIDARIES[46] .... - 65 -

Diamond .... - 65 -

Sapphire .... - 65 -

Amethyst .... - 66 -

Chelidonius .... - 66 -

Coral .... - 66 -

Heliotrope .... - 67 -

- PEARL ....- 67 -
- PANTHEROS ....- 67 -
- SYMBOLISM OF THE CARBUNCLE[47] ....- 67 -
- SYMBOLISM OF THE TWELVE STONES[48] ....- 68 -

HOMILY ....- 69 -

- CONCERNING MIRACLE PLAYS, GAMES, AND MINSTRELSY[49] ....- 69 -

SATIRE ....- 71 -

- THE SONG OF THE UNIVERSITY OF PARIS[51] ....- 71 -
- THE LAND OF COCKAYGNE[52] ....- 73 -
- THE COMPLAINT OF THE HUSBANDMAN[53] ....- 75 -
- SIR PENNY[63] ....- 77 -

LAY ....- 83 -

- SIR ORFEO[64] ....- 83 -

NOTES ....- 103 -

- Frontispiece ....- 103 -
- PROEM ....- 103 -
- DEBATE ....- 103 -
- VISION ....- 105 -

SAINTS' LIVES .... - 107 -

PIOUS TALES.. - 108 -

ALLEGORY .... - 109 -

BESTIARY .... - 111 -

LAPIDARY .... - 112 -

HOMILY... - 113 -

SATIRE... - 114 -

LAY .... - 116 -

FOOTNOTES: .... - 118 -

PREFACE

This volume of translations is prepared especially for the use of college sophomores who are studying English poetry of the fourteenth century, but it is hoped that other readers may be interested in these old legends. Ideally, it would be better for students to read the original texts, but every teacher knows how difficult it is to provide texts in this field. The various Middle English Readers are not frankly popular in their choice of subject matter, and the publications of learned societies are far too expensive to be available for classroom work. It does not seem, therefore, entirely an offense against scholarship to offer students a volume that will serve humbly as companion to "Piers Plowman," "The Pearl," Chaucer's poems, and various romances and lyrics which are studied in carefully edited texts.

The modern translations are literal, but a certain freedom has been used in reshaping sentences and in omitting conventional phrases when they proved too monotonous in their repetitions. Quite enough *tags* and awkward constructions have been preserved to illustrate fully the style of mediæval clerks.

Acknowledgment is made for help received from Gaston Paris's "La littérature française au moyen âge," and from W. H. Schofield's "English Literature from the Norman Conquest to Chaucer." Miss Marion E. Markley has contributed two translations from Old French, and has given many helpful suggestions regarding details.

M. H. S.

WELLESLEY, MASSACHUSETTS

INTRODUCTION

To create anew the walls and towers and gardens of the mediæval world is a comparatively easy task, now that we have so many aids to visualizing that departed age, but it is not so easy to make live again the thoughts and sentiments and beliefs of a vanished generation. All our study of history is valueless unless it brings a clearer revelation of the pulsing, ardent life of humanity. We search old records and old literature that we may find the true image of a world whose hopes and fears and loves prove to us the slow evolution of a progressive civilization in which all human beings share. Out of the failures and the doubts of one age comes the quicker power of another, and true progress looks both backward and forward. To cherish old traditions is both a duty and an inspiration.

The reader who turns his face toward the world of mediæval England and France, seeking to know the spirit which animated our ancestors of six centuries ago, must recognize in plowman, hermit, knight, friar, or minstrel the fundamental fact that their life was actual and real, not a mere tissue of mediæval costume and mechanical movements. In order to understand that epoch it is essential for one to study in detail the works which picture the life of the day. The world of chivalry, with its brilliant pageantry and its vows of courtesy, loyalty, and liberality, is revealed in the pages of Froissart and in the many metrical romances, where various aspects of knightly life are described. "King Horn," "Guy of Warwick," "Libeaus Desconus," "Sir Eglamour," "The Squire of Low Degree," and others tell the story of knighthood.

Another world is represented in "Piers Plowman," where the oppression of the poor by the arrogant rich and the corruption of church and state are described in racy vernacular by one whose soul was on fire with devotion to truth and justice. Social problems are enunciated, and the misery wrought by human ignorance and selfishness is depicted in satire keen, shrewd, and piercing.

Chaucer, the supreme poet of the fourteenth century in England, portrays a world of normal folk who represent all classes and conditions except the very high and the very low. While, in certain ways, Chaucer's work is easier to read and understand than that of any of his contemporaries, students often read it very superficially and fail to recognize the deeply rooted traits which show that Chaucer was the child of his epoch. We find in the English poet traces of the influence of Continental life and literature; we see him reading the classics of Rome, of Florence, and of Paris; but he was also always intimately familiar with the minor literature popular among his own countrymen.

Since an understanding of Chaucer is a vivid introduction to the later Middle Ages, it is essential for students of that period to have some acquaintance with the common literary types of Chaucer's day. The translations gathered together in this book are representative of these types,—debate, vision, allegory, saints' legends, pious tales, satire, and lay. Few examples of secular literature are given, for the most satisfactory way to approach the secular poetry of the time is to read parts, at least, of the "Romance of the Rose," which has been translated, very freely, by F. S. Ellis.[1] This long poem is a compendium of the ideals, manners, and tastes of the fashionable world of France and of England. The machinery of dream, personification, and allegory; the descriptions of nature and of dress; the attitude towards the god of love and his fabled court; the satire; and the pedantry are all highly significant facts in the history of literature. Knowing this romance, one knows the heart of thirteenth century Paris. The Troubadours,[2] too, should be studied for the sake of understanding one side of lyric poetry. All this secular poetry, however, does not account for Chaucer, who was indebted also to a stream of influence coming from religious legends and allegories. The deeper side of his nature responded to the appeal of pious tales and records of saintly lives; superstitions about nature and about God attracted his interest, and stirred him to that effective contemplation which resulted in clear, sane judgments. Religious poetry was, first and last, familiar matter to the great court poet, and we should recognize its characteristics and its sovereign appeal.

We must remember that the world of the Middle Ages was essentially and positively Catholic. From birth to death the layman was under the guardianship of Holy Church, and bound by the most solemn vows to perfect obedience. Yet, although there seems to be a certain conventionality in his performance of these duties, there was a very lively concern regarding that other world toward which he was moving. Close to the spiritual ecstasy of such lives as that of Saint Francis, or of Saint Catherine, or of the uncanonized Richard Rolle, there was a dim, frightened foreboding that perhaps Evil might prove the triumphant force. Love of God was no stronger than fear of the devil. Tales of the black magic of Satan as well as of the white magic of the church were eagerly listened to by a people quick to show their interest in any manifestation of the supernatural. Crude and childish as their faiths and superstitions may seem to a more liberal age, there is something impressive in their deep conviction of hidden truths. When we lose all sense of mystery and of wonder and are wholly free from any illusions, life becomes singularly vapid, for the very key to spiritual existence is a sense of infinite meanings forever challenging, baffling, and dominating our daily life.

"But God forbede but men shulde leve

Wel more thing then men han seen with ÿe!"

In the legends and allegories and satires represented in these pages the reader will find strange and fervent faiths as well as homely pictures of the world as it is. A vigorous use of the concrete is everywhere evident; abstractions seem not to exist without some physical traits to make them real to the ordinary man. Intensely picturesque and objective are the descriptions of hell and of heaven, of the lands visited by Brandon, of Saint Paul's otter, of the miracles of Saint Thomas, of the virtues of the coral, and of the traits of Rose and of Violet. To any readers there is unending charm in the natural, simple style of setting forth these details which force vivid conceptions upon the imagination.

Growing up in a world of brilliant court life and becoming familiar with a literary art which placed emphasis upon the concrete, Chaucer was inevitably destined to be a supreme master of specific, suggestive realism. He loved every aspect of existence, and he wrought his descriptions with an art precise and joyous. The French poets and the English preachers taught him the secret of appealing to the popular love of visible and audible images. Yet his greatest power is that dramatic portrayal of human experience, a presentation whose quick humour and overflowing sympathy have made him beloved by generations. Impatient of affectation in art, in manner, or in spiritual matters, he taught sincerity. His humour, poise, and fearless, keen mentality will always have their healing and wonder-working qualities.

PROEM

OF MAN'S BODY[3]

As I said before, the King of Might would be worshipped by two kinds of beings, angel and man. Adam was created, therefore, to make the tenth order, which Lucifer tried to destroy. Adam was not made of earth alone, but of four elements: his blood of water, his flesh of earth, his heat of fire, and his breath of air. His head has two eyes. The sky has sun and moon that, as men know, are set for sight; so man's eyes serve as sun and moon of light. Seven chief stars are fixed in heaven, and man's head has seven holes, which, if you think about it, you may find with little labor. This breath that man draws so often betokens the wind that blows aloft, of which thunder and lightning are created, as breath is bred in the breast with a cough. All waters sink into the sea, so man's stomach drinks all liquors. His feet bear him up from falling, as the earth upholds all things. The upper fire gives man his sight, the upper air his power of hearing, the under wind gives him his breath, the earth gives him his taste, feeling, and touch; the hardness of bone that man has comes to him from the nature of stones. From the earth grow trees and grass; and from man's flesh, nails and hair. With dumb beasts man has his share of things which he likes ill or well. Of these things, I have heard said, Adam's body was put together. For this reason that you have heard, man is called the lesser world.

OF MAN'S SOUL

But you have not yet heard the story of how man's soul was wrought. A ghostly light man says it is that God has made in His likeness; as print of a seal is fixed in wax, so man has God's likeness. He has wrought him as friend and companion, since nothing is so dear to Him. His Godhead is the Trinity, so a soul has properly three powers: the perception of what is, was, and shall be. It has pure understanding of what is seen and is unseen; it has, also, wisdom of will to take the good and leave the evil. All the powers that may be dwell in that Holy Trinity. That soul which is cleansed from sin has all virtues.

As God, who is one and three, may by no kind of creature be understood nor overtaken, but He overtakes each one, so the soul, without spot, is unseen, though it has sight of all things. To see the soul you have no power. Now have I shown you how two things hold man together;—the soul, a thing spiritual, and the body, which is flesh and skin.

Translated by M. H. S.

DEBATE

THE AMOROUS CONTENTION OF PHILLIS AND FLORA[4]

In flowry season of the yeere,
And when the firmament was cleere,
When Tellus hierbales paynted were
With issue of disparent[5] chere.

When th'usher to the morne did rise,
And drive the darknes from the skyes,
Sleepe gave their visuale liberties
To Phillis and to Floras eyes.

To walke these Ladyes liked best,
For sleepe rejects the wounded brest,
Who joyntly to a meade addrest,
Their sportance with the place to feast.

Thus made they amorous accesse,
Both virgins and both princesces;
Fayre Phillis wore a liberal tresse,
But Flora hirs in curls did dresse.

Nor in their ornamentall grace,
Nor in behaviour were they bace;
Their yeeres and mindes in egall[6] place
Did youth and his effects embrace.

A little yet unlike they proove,

And somewhat hostilely they strove:
A scholler Floras minde did moove,
But Phillis likt a souldiers love.

For stature and fresh bewties flowrs,
There grew no difference in their dowrs,
All thinges were free to both their powrs
Without and in their courtly bowrs.

One vow they made religiously,
And were of one societie;
And onely was their impacie[7]
The forme of eithers phantasie.[8]

Now did a timely gentle gale
A little whisper through the dale,
Where was a place of festivale,
With verdant grasse adorned all.

And in that meade-prowd-making grasse,
A river, like to liquid glasse,
Did in such sound-full murmure passe,
That with the same it wanton was.

Hard by this brooke a pyne had seate,
With goodly furniture compleate,
To make the place in state more greate
And lessen the inflaming heate.

Which was with leaves so bewtifide
 And spread his brest so thicke and wide,
That all the sunnes estranged pride
Sustainde repulse on every side.

Fayre Phillis by the foorde did sit,
But Flora far remov'd from it,
The place in all thinges sweete was fit,
Where herbage did their seates admit.

Thus milde they opposite were set,
And coulde not their affects forget,
Loves arrows and their bosoms met,
And both their harts did passion fret.

Love close and inward shrowds his fires,
And in faint words firme sighs enspires,
Pale tinctures change their cheeks attires,
But modest shame entoombs their ires.

Phillis did Flora sighing take,
And Flora did requitale make:
So both together part the stake,
Till foorth the wound and sicknes brak.

In this chang'd speech they long time staide,
The processe all on Love they laide,
Love in their harts their lookes bewraide,
At last in laughter Phillis saide:

"Brave souldier," sayd she, "O my Paris,
In fight, or where so ere he tarries,
The souldiers lyfe lyfes glory carries,
Onely worth Venus household quarries."[9]

While she hir warr-friende did prefer,
Flora lookt coye and laught at her;
And did this adverse speech aver:

"Thou shouldst have said, I love a begger.

"But what doth he my hart embraces?
A thing create, that all things passes,
Whom nature blest with all hir graces;
O clerkes, in you blisse all blisse places."

This hard speech Phillis hardly takes,
And thus she Floras pacience crakes;
"Thou lov'st a man pure love forsakes,
That God his godles bellie makes.

"Rise, wretch, from this grosse extasie,
A clerke sole epicure thinke I.
No elegance can bewtifie
A shapeles lump of gluttonie.

"His hart sweete Cupids tents rejects,
That onely meate and drinke affects:
O Flora, all mens intelects
Know souldiers vows, shun those respects.

"Meere helpes for neede his minde suffiseth,
 Dull sleepe and surfetts he despiseth,
Loves trump his temples exerciseth,
Cooradge and love, his life compriseth.

"Who with like band our loves combineth?
Even Natures law thereat repineth;
My love in conquests palme-wreths shineth,
Thine feasts deforms, mine fight refineth."

Flora hir modest face enrosed,
Whose second smile more fayre disclosed,

At length with mooving voyce she losed
What art in her storde brest reposed.

"Phillis, thy fill of speech thou hast,
Thy witt with pointed wings is grast,
Yet urdgest not a trueth so vast,
That hemlocks lillies have surpast.

"Ease loving clerkes thou holdst for cleere,
Servants to sloth and bellie cheere;
So envie honor would enpheere,[10]
But give me eare, Ile give thee answere.

"So much enjoyes this love of myne,
He nere envies, or hirs, or thyne;
Household stuffe, honny, oyle, corne, wine,
Coyne, jewels, plate, serve his designe.

"Such pleasing store have clerks bylying,
 As none can fayne their dignifying:
There, Love clasps his glad wings in flying,
Love ever firme, Love never dying.

"Loves stings in him are still sustained,
Yet is my clerke nor pinde nor pained:
Joy hath no part in him restrained,
To whom his love beares thoughts unfained.

"Palled, and leane, is thy elected,
Poore, scarce with cloths or skin contected,
His sinews weake, his brest dyjected,
For nothing causde maks nought effected.

"Approching neede is Loves meere hell,

Souldiers want gyfts to woo loves well:
But clerks give much, and still heaps swell,
Their rents and riches so excell."

"Right well thou knowst" (Phillis replide)
"What in both arts and lyves abide,
Likely, and clenly thou hast lide:
But thus our difference is not tride.

"When holy-day the whole world cheeres,
A clerke lifes modest figure beares:
His crowne is heaven, black weeds he weares,
And showes a mind halfe dround in teares.

"None is so poore of sence or eyne,
To whom a souldier doth not shyne:
At ease, like sprightles beasts lives thyne,
Helms, and barb'd horse, do weare out myne.

"Mine low with armes makes foe-towrs ly,
And when on foote he fight doth try,
While his fayre squire his horse holds by,
Mine thinks on me, and then they dy.

"He turns, fight past, and foes inchased,
And lookes on me with helme unlaced,
Lifts his strong lyms, and brest strait graced,
And saies, kyss-blesse me, O hart-placed."

Flora her wrath in pants did spye,
And many a dart at hir lets flye:
"Thou canst not make with heaven-reacht crye
A camel pierce a needels eye.

"False goes for true, for honny, gall,
To make a clerke a souldiers thrall;
Doth love to souldiers coradge call?
No, but the neede they toyle withall.

"Fayre Phillis, would thy love were wise,
No more the trueth to contrarise!
Hunger and thirst bow souldiers thies,
In which Deaths path and Plutos lies.

"Sharpe is the wasting bane of warre
The lot is hard, and strayneth farre:
The lyfe is stooping, doubts doth jarre,
To get such things as needefull are.

"Knewst thou the case, thou wouldst not say,
Shaven haire sham'd clerks, or black aray:
Worne higher honors to display,
And that all states they oversway.

"All things should to my clerke encline,
Whose crowne sustains th' impereal signe;
He rules and payes such friendes as thine,
And lay must stoope to men divine.

"Thou sayst that sloth a clerke disguiseth,
Who I confesse base workes despiseth:
But when from cares his free minde riseth,
Heavens course and Naturs he compriseth.

"Mine purple decks, thine maile bedighteth,
Thine lives in war, mine peace delighteth,
Olde acts of princes he resighteth,

All of his friend thinks, seeks, and wrighteth.

"What Venus can, or Loves wingd lord,
First knowes my clerke, and brings me word:
Musicke in cares doth mine afford,
Thine joyes in rapine and the sword."

Here speech and strife had both their ending,
Phillis askt judgment, all suspending:
Much stir they made, yet ceast contending;
And sought a judge in homewards wending.

With countnances that egale[11] beene,
With egale majestie beseene:
With egale voyce, and egale spleene,
These virgins ward uppon the greene.

Phillis a white robe bewtifide,
Flora wore one of two hews dide:
Phillis upon a mule did ride,
Flora did back a horse of pride.

The mule was that which being create,
Neptune did feede, and subjugate:
Which after fayre Adonis fate,
He Venus sent to cheere hir state.

This, she the queene of Iberine,
Phillis fayre mother did resigne,
Since she was given to workes divine,
Whence Phillis had the mule in fine.

Who of the trappings asks, and bit,
The mule (though silver) champing it:

Know all things were so richly fit,
As Neptunes honor might admit.

Then Phillis no decorid wanted,
 But rich and bewtious, all eyes daunted:
Nor Floras vertue lesse enchaunted,
Who on a welthy palfrey vaunted.

Tamde with his raines, won heaven for lightnes,
Exceeding fayre, and full of wightnes,[12]
His brest art dectt with divers brightnes,
For jeate blacke mixt with swans pure whightnes.

Young and in dainty shape dygested,
His lookes with pride, not rage, invested:
His mayne thin haird, his neck high crested,
Small eare, short head, and burly brested.

His brode backe stoopt to this clerks-loved,
Which with hir pressure nought was moved:
Strait legd, large thighd, and hollow hoved,
All Natures skill in him was proved.

An ivorie seate on him had place,
A hoope of golde did it imbrace,
Graven: and the poitrell[13] did enchace
A stone that star-like gave it grace.

Inscription there allurde the eye,
With many a wondrous misterie:
Of ancient thinges made noveltie,
That never man did yet descrie.

The God of Rhetoriques nuptiall bowre,

Adornd with every heavenly powre,
The contract, and the mariage howre,
And all the most unmeasurd dowre.

No place was there that figurd nought,
That could through all the world be sought:
But more excesse of mervails wrought,
Then might inceede[14] a humane thought.

The skyll of Mulciber alone
Engrav'd that admirable throne:
Who looking stedfastly thereon,
Scarse thought his hand such art had shone.

The trappings wrought he not with ease,
But all his payne employde to please:
And left, to go in hand with these,
The tardge of great Aeacides.[15]

A styrrop for hir feete to presse,
And bridle-bosses he did dresse,
And added rains in worths excesse,
Of his sweete spowses goulden tresse.

Thus on their famouse cavalrye,
These prince-borne damzels seemd to flye:
Their soft young cheekebales to the eye
Are of the fresh vermilion dye.

So lillies out of scarlet peere,
So roses of the vernall yeere,
So shoote two wanton starrs y-feere[16]
From the eternall burning spheere.

The child-gods gracefull paradise,
They joyntly purpose to invise:[17]
And lovely emulations rise,
In note of one anothers guise.

Phillis to Flora, laughter led,
And Flora Phillis answered:
A merlin Phillis managed,
A sparhawlke Flora caried.

In little tyme these ladyes founde
A grove with every pleasure crounde:
At whose sweete entrie did resounde
A foorde that flowrd that holy grounde.

From thence the sweete-breathd winds convay
Odors from every mirtle spray:
And other flowrs, to whose aray
A hundred harpes and timbrels play.

All pleasurs studie can invent,
The dames eares instantly present:
Voyces in all sorts different,
The foure parts, and the diapent.[18]

Two tunes that from those voyces flie,
 With admirable harmonie:
The tymbrell, harpe, and psalterie,
Rejoyce in rapting symphonie.

There did the vials voyce abounde,
In musicke angel-like profounde:
There did the phife dispredden rounde

His songe in many a variant sounde.

All birdes with tunefull bosoms sing,
The blackbird makes the woods to ring:
The thrush, the jay, and she[19] in spring
Rues the past rape of Thraces king.

Their shrill notes to the musicke plying,
Then all the different flowrs descrying,
The odors in abundance flying,
Prov'd it the bowre of Loves soft-lying.

The virgins something entered here,
And sprinckled with a little feare,
Their harts before that helde Love deare,
In Cupids flames encreased were.

And while each winged forester
Their proper rumors[20] did prefer,
Each virgins minde made waight on her
Applauses apt and singuler.

Deathles were he coulde there repose,
 Each path his spycie odor stroes:
Of mirh and synamon there groes,
And of our blessed Ladyes rose.

Each tree hath there his severall blisse,
In fruites that never season misse:
Men may conceave how sweete Love is,
By that celestiall court of his.

The dauncing companies they see
Of young men and of maydens free;

Whose bodyes are as bright in blee,[21]
As starrs illustrate bodyes bee.

In which so mervaylous a guyse
Of unexpected novelties,
These virgins bosoms through their eyes
Were daunted with a quicke surprise.

Who stay their royall steads outright,
And almost from their seates alight:
Forgetting their endevors quight,
With that proud rumors sweete affright.

But when sad Philomene did straine
Her rape-full-raving brest againe,
These ladyes hearing hir complaine,
Were reinflamd in every vaine.

About the center of the spring,
 A secret place is where they sing,
And use their supreme worshypping,
Of Loves neare-darting fiery king.

There many a two-shapt companie,
Of faunes, nimphes, satyres, meete and plie
The tymbrell and the psalterie,
Before Loves sacred majestie.

There beare they goblets bigg with wine,
And coronets of flowrs combine:
There nimphs and fauns demy-divine,
Doth Bacchus teach to foote it fine.

Who keepe true measure with their feete,

That to the instruments do fleete:
But olde Silenus playes not sweete
In consort, but indents the streete.[22]

The spring-sleepe did his temples lode,
As on a long-eard asse he rode:
Laughters excesse, to see him nod,
Dissolv'd the bosome of the God.

Fresh cups he ever cals uppon,
In sounds of imperfection,
With age and Bacchus overgon,
They stop his voyces organon.

Amongst this gamesome crew is seene,
 The issue of the Cyprian Queene,
Whose head and shoulders fethered beene,
And as the starrs his countnance sheene.

In his left hand his bow he bare,
And by his side his quiver ware:
In powre he sits past all compare,
And with his flames the worlde doth dare.

A scepter in his hand he hild,
With Chloris native flowrs untild,
And nectars deathles odors stild,
From his bright lookes the sunne did guild.

The triple Graces there assist,
Supporting with their brests commist,
And knees that Tellus bosome kist,
The challice of this amorist.

These ladyes now approched neare,
And worshipped exempt from feare
Loves god: who was environd there
With youth, that honord stiles did beare.

Their joy is superexcellent,
To see a court so confluent:
Whom Cupid, seeing their intent,
Doth with his greeting intervent.

He askes the cause for which they came:
They confidently tell the same:
And he gives prayse to eyther dame,
That durst so great a warre proclame.

To both he spake to make some pause,
Untyll their honorable cause,
Profoundly wayde in every clause,
Might be explande with all applause.

He was a God which well they know,
Rehearsall needes it not bestow:
They light and rest, and playnely show,
Where Love strives, Love wil maister grow.

Love lawes and judges hath in fee,[23]
Nature and use his judges bee:
To whom his whole courts censures flee,
Since past, and things to come, they see.

These do the hart of justice trie,
And show the courts severitie:
In judgment, and strong customs eye,

The clerke is fitst for venerie.[24]

Gainst which the queenes but little strove,
Since Loves high voyce did it approve:
So both to their abodes remove:
But as at first, rest firm in Love.

Translated by George Chapman(?)

THE PLEADING OF THE ROSE AND OF THE VIOLET[25]

In the presence of Imagination, before whom in due course of law actions are brought, an argument was one day commenced between the Rose and the Violet. The matter, of which I treat, was most wisely conducted. To set forth fully points, process, articles, and case, the advocate of the Rose appeared first and began as follows:

"Violet! I am here to propound a question in behalf of my lady, lovely Rose; I hereby announce to you, and intend likewise to proclaim and sustain in all courts of the land, that Rose is of greater worth, more desired, and more dearly esteemed than you are. That is just, for indeed she adorns the season with her color, more delicate than purple and crimson, and with her sweet fragrance. She lasts much longer in her beauty than do you, Violet; and, red or white, she springs in the pleasant month of May to draw all lovers out of their sadness. Then do ladies and youths, lords, bachelors and maidens gather her flowers, some making chaplets of them and others weaving garlands to adorn themselves."

At this point, the advocate of the Violet, who was very old, could no longer keep silent, and broke in:

"O God! If I did not know how to speak, I might have to withdraw from this argument, but, if it please God, I shall speak, and I shall support the cause of Violet against Rose. Sir Advocate, I say and affirm, in spite of your speech, that Violet is more joyfully welcomed, more beloved, and more desired than Rose. Here is the cause; now listen to the truth. When a winter full of frost and chill shall have put to rout, by its prolonged stay, trees and fruits, leaves and flowers, then men and women and children long for bright days, and wish the springtime to come swiftly, when they will hear the singing of larks and will find violets in orchards, gardens, and every pretty close. There youths and maidens gather them and make gay chaplets, and many put them under their pillows in token of delight and pleasure. And when this sweet and fresh season of spring comes anew, you may see many people fastening violets in fresh green sprays of gooseberry, and arranging them so as to set off their beauty and fragrance. To speak truly, Sir Advocate, one cannot do them too much honor. Now, I pray you, sit down; for I would rest a little. But I will take up the argument again, if, indeed, there be any further need of my services."

Each of the advocates seated himself, and Imagination set a day for their return, for she wished to hear them further.

Here follows how the Advocate of the Rose sets forth her Cause

Now they have come to the appointed day; may it dawn happily, for I would hear most gladly the order of their discourse. The advocate of the Rose spoke first, for he was well versed in speaking, and he addressed them as follows:

"Before Imagination, who is my sovereign lady, I here make protest and vigorous complaint against the grievous charges with which Violet oppresses us. When she wishes to detract from the power of the Rose, white and red, she shows little discrimination, and her advocate likewise, for as black differs from white so it is clear the Violet differs from the Rose. I do not know who is counselling this advocate, but certainly he is not endowed with good judgment; or if he is, it does not appear in this case. Now, to silence him completely I will give some details, that he may take counsel of them. First of all, I will compare the red rose, by figure, to the sun, for the round sun, when we see it rising at morning and setting at night, is in color not at all variegated, but sanguine indeed, and deep red as the red rose. There are yet further considerations why one should greatly honor the Rose. You know that there are two kinds of grapes, from which are made white wine and red, and with these wines the holy sacrament is solemnly celebrated. I choose the white rose to stand for the white wine, and for red wine the red rose. Indeed, they still cry in the streets, 'Come buy the good wine *Rosette*.' Roses, white and red, have mysterious and agreeable virtue, for from them is made a liquid, called rose water, that is good for healthy folk, and necessary for those that are ill, because it assuages strong fevers. It is refreshing to the face, and to the mouth and the hands. Many, indeed, wish their pillows, be it for sleeping or waking, may be scented with the fragrance of the Rose. Consider where the Rose dwells. I call the rose-bush her house. God set her there, in all reason, not shut up in a tower, but enclosed about with sharp thorns so that the young goats that love to pasture on violets and nibble the leaves and tender shoots shall not touch roses nor buds."

With this, the advocate for the Rose was silent, having reviewed wisely and well, it seemed, the case of the Rose, red and white. The court adjourned for a little, until there was great impatience to know if the advocate of the Violet, having heard the case for lovely Rose, would return to the debate. Truly, you shall hear how he responded with much wisdom. But I must write down his replies before I can recite them.

Here follows how the Advocate of the Violet sustains her Cause

"O Advocate for Violet, come forward, for they bring points of opposition against you," said Imagination, "and you will have to make reply to them, unless I am to dismiss the case."

The advocate answered, "Lady, I am all ready, by my soul, to reply, and to do my duty, and to show that I have spoken truth. First of all, I state, in plain prose, that I do not doubt the Rose may be beautiful and good and wise and may have many ways and uses that are much to be commended; but I should like to ask her advocate if his figure of the sun is acceptable or quite truthful. The Rose is cool and moist, the sun hot; now, in this point, his argument is false. However, let that count for what it may. My sword is as sharpened for all thrusts as his. He is foolish who evades his opponent when he can attack him. I have both occasion and motive for challenging him, and so I do it. He has just now compared the Rose to the sun; I assure him that I will not, by a still worse figure, compare violets to the stars or the planets. I will not strain his comparison farther, for that would be foolish. But I will name them daughters of the round firmament, for they have her own color, without white, black, red, or green. When clouds came down from the heavens, the earth drank in their moisture and conceived violets, so she holds them in deep affection. Blue signifies steadfastness; he or she who wears it, remember, must have a heart always firm and steadfast and strengthened. Violets are flowers of good worth, fair to see and to wear. When ladies and maidens have fine gowns or rich hangings for their beds, if they scent them with violets people will say, 'This robe is sweet,' and will enjoy the odor. Violets, dear masters, have further power and virtue, which strengthens my argument and overthrows all your specious comments.

"Take violets and roses, and, to test their power, throw them into brandy, to see what will happen and what will become of their odor. The brandy, which is powerful, will take away substance and vigor from the lovely Rose, while the Violet will persist in its fragrance; this is certain. So I hold her, and with reason, to be of far greater importance and of much nobler quality than the Rose. Furthermore, there is made from violets a good lotion which gives comfort to sick people, and from the plants and roots are made several medicines, but you cannot make anything out of a rose-bush, except a fire in winter. And if goats or sheep do browse on violets, I am sure that the milk they give does much good to the children who drink it."

Then Master Papin, the advocate of the Rose, stood up and wished to say something, but Imagination spoke before him, and said, "Where are you going, Sir Advocate? You weary us with so much talking. Who wants to listen to your speeches? They would fill four rolls. We must stop your pleading, for we are compelled to hear other cases."

"Lady," said the advocate, "you ought to hear all suits out; for that is your court open. Do not be so hasty; you complain of the debate too soon. Pronounce your just decision on our case."

Imagination, at these words, declared that she would hear no more, nor would she give a decision.

"Who will then? Tell us that, Lady!"

"Willingly," she replied; "you have elsewhere a court of appeal for judging right and wrong, which is higher than mine."

"And where is it? Lead us to it, or direct us, and we will go there."

Imagination replied, "Good sir Advocate, the noble and high Fleur-de-lys, whom men should hold in dear esteem, has sovereignty, has she not, over the Rose and all other flowers? Indeed she has and always has had and shall have, as is just; for as the lion is king of beasts and the eagle king of birds, so, I assure you, is the Fleur-de-lys sovereign lady over all flowers, and most exalted. Therefore go to her court,—happy is he who has recourse to it,—I cannot send you to a better place to plead your cause. The way is not very long; say that I sent you there for counsel, that they may help you."

"Ah, dear lady, and where does the Fleur-de-lys live? Since this is so, we will go there, if it please you."

She responds, without hesitation, "In the noble realm of France. There you will find with all delight the noble and high Fleur-de-lys surrounded in state by a fair and goodly company: Hardihood, Youth, Wisdom, Honor, and Largesse, by whom you will be welcomed gladly and advised with counsel gracious and wise. For the King, Orleans and Bourbon, Berry, Bourgoyne, Eu, and La Marche will not break their promise to study wisely, to consider loyally, and to examine your dispute, which will be pleasing to them. And when they have heard it, I believe that they will answer so wisely and so to the point that there will never be more argument between Rose and Violet such as this plea deals with. And if, through any difficulty in the affair, it should be necessary to have counsel, you know there are still the

Marguerites, small and beautiful flowers, whom it is a pleasure to meet again at all seasons, summer and winter, and there are several other noble flowers, with which her court is much adorned, who may give her faithful counsel. Go there, I advise you."

"Lady," said he, "that is our purpose." With that the hearing was closed.

Translated by Marion E. Markley

VISION

THE PURGATORY OF SAINT PATRICK[26]

Saint Patrick felt such pity for the Irish folk, who lived in deadly sin and false belief, that he constantly besought them to turn to God and obey His law, but they were so full of wickedness that they scorned every word he spoke. They all said that they would not repent nor cease from evil unless he would undertake the adventure of going down into hell to bring them back tidings of the pain and woe which souls suffer there evermore. The saint was sorely dismayed upon hearing this, and, often, with fasting and prayer, he begged Jesus Christ to grant him the grace to find a way by which he might bring the people of Ireland out of bondage to the fiend, and lead them to believe in God Omnipotent.

Once, while he was in holy church, praying thus, he fell asleep before the altar, and began to dream of heaven's bliss; he thought that Jesus came to him and gave him a book such as no clerk can ever write, telling all manner of good tidings of heaven and earth and hell, and of God's mystery. Into his hand God put a fair staff, which to this day is called, in Ireland, God's staff. And God led him straightway thence into a great desert where was a secret opening, grisly to see. Round it was, and black; in all the world it has no mate. When Saint Patrick saw that sight he was greatly troubled in his sleep, but God revealed to him that if a man who had sinned against the holy law and yet truly repented should do penance in this hole, a day and a night, his sins would be forgiven him. If the man were of good faith, steadfast in belief, he should see the strong pains of those who have sinned in this world, but should not suffer himself, and finally, he should behold the joy that lasts for aye in paradise. Then Jesus withdrew his gracious countenance and left Patrick there alone.

When the saint awoke he found God's tokens, and, taking them in his hand, he knelt to thank Jesus Christ for revealing to him how he might turn the Irish folk to amendment. On that spot, without delay, he had a fair abbey built, in the name of God and of our Lady. The abbey had no equal anywhere; solace and glee and rejoicing abounded for poor and for rich. White canons regular were placed there to serve God early and late and to be holy men. The book and the staff God gave him men may still see. In the east end of the abbey is that grisly hole, with a good stone wall all around it, and a gate with lock and key. That very spot is called the right entrance to Patrick's Purgatory, for in the times when this happened many a man went down to hell, as the story tells us, and suffered pain for his trespasses, and then returned again, through God's grace. They all said, when they had come out, that they had indeed seen the very pains of hell and also the joys of angels singing to God and to his hosts. That is the joy of paradise: Jesus bring us thither! When the people of Ireland began to understand the joys described by Saint Patrick, they all came to him and were christened at the font and forsook their misdeeds. So they became good Christians through knowledge of God and the prayers of Saint Patrick. Now hearken, and I will tell you about another thing, if you care to hear it.

In the days of Stephen, a king who ruled England wisely, there was in Northumberland a knight who was a brave and valiant man. He was born in that country, and was called Owain. He knew much about battle, and he was very sinful towards his Creator. One day, bethinking himself of his sins, he was filled with dread, and he determined, through God's grace, to be shriven and sin no more. By chance, he came to the Bishop of Ireland, in that abbey where the hole of penance was, and he confessed and prayed that a sore penance be laid upon him, for never again, he said, would he sin. The bishop was glad of this promise, and, after rebuking Owain sharply for his evil deeds, said that he must undertake many hard tasks of penance. The knight answered, "Gladly will I do what God ordains, though it be to go into Patrick's Purgatory." The bishop, describing to him the torments of the place, said, "Nay, friend Owain, that way thou shalt not go. Take some other penance in expiation of thy sins." However, for all the bishop could say the knight would not yield, so the bishop led him into the holy church and taught him the law of God.

Fifteen days he spent in affliction, in fasting, and in prayer, and then the prior, at the head of a procession with cross and banner, brought him to the hole. The prior said, "Knight Owain, here is thy way, go right forward; when thou hast proceeded a long distance and hast lost the light of day, still keep directly north. Thou shalt go thus under the earth, and then, very soon, thou wilt find a great field where there is a hall of stone, unlike any other in the world. Some light there is, but no more than appears when the sun goes to ground in winter. Into that hall thou shalt go and stay until folk come to solace thee. Thirteen[27] men will appear, all serjeants of God, and they will counsel thee about thy course through purgatory."

Then the prior and the convent commended him to God and went forth, shutting the gate. The knight took the way leading to the field where was the hall of stone. The hall was the work of no earthly workman; it was cleverly made in fashion of a cloister, with pillars on each side. When the knight had stood a long time, marvelling, he entered. Soon, thirteen wise men appeared, all dressed in white habits and with their heads newly tonsured. Their leader, advancing, saluted the knight, and then sat down to instruct him: "I shall counsel thee, dear brother, as I have many another who has passed this way, to be of good faith, certain, and without doubt, for thou wilt see, when we have departed, a thousand fiends and more to lead thee to torment; take note that if thou dost obey them in the slightest thing, thy soul will be lost. Keep God in thy heart, and think how He suffered from His wounds. Unless thou dost as I tell thee, thou wilt go to hell, body and soul, and be lost eternally. If thou dost speak God's high name, they cannot harm thee." When he had thus counselled the knight, the leader and his fellows commended him to God, and with benign looks went forth from the hall.

Owain, left there in dread, began to lament and call upon God. Soon he heard a piteous cry; he could not have been more frightened if the heaven had fallen. When he had recovered from the fear caused by that cry, there came flocking in a crowd of fiends, fifty score or more, loathsome things altogether. Crowding around the knight they laughed him to scorn, saying that he had come in flesh and skin to win the joys of hell forever. The master fiend, falling upon his knees, said, "Welcome, Owain; thou art come to suffer penance for thy sins, but thou wilt get no benefit, for thou shalt have torments, hard and strong and tough enough because of thy deadly sins. Never hadst thou more mischance than thou shalt have in our dance when we begin our sport. However, if thou wilt do our bidding, since thou art dear to us, our whole company will bring thee back with tender love to the spot where thou didst leave the prior. If thou dost refuse, we shall prove to thee that thou hast served us many a year in pride and luxury, and all our company will thrust their hooks at thee." Owain answered, "I forsake your counsel, and will endure my penance." When the fiends heard this, they made a great fire in the hall, and binding him fast, feet and hands, they cast him into the midst of it. He called upon our Lord, and at once the fire vanished; no coal nor spark was left, through the grace of God Almighty. As soon as the knight saw this he grew bolder, realizing that it was the treachery of the fiends to try his heart.

Then the devils went out of the hall, leading the knight with them to a strange place, where nothing good entered, only hunger, thirst, and cold. He could see no tree, could hear no sound of wind, yet a cold blast blew that pierced his side. At last the fiends brought him to a valley where the knight thought he must have reached the deepest pit of hell. As he drew nearer, he looked about, for he heard screaming and groaning, and he saw a field full of men and women, each lying face downward, naked, and with deadly wounds. They lay prone on the earth, bound with iron bands, screaming and wailing, "Alas, alas, mercy, mercy, mercy, God Almighty!" Mercy there was none, but only sorrow of heart and grinding of teeth, which was a grisly sight. That sorrow and misery is punishment for the foul sin of sloth. Whosoever is slow in God's service may expect to lie in purgatory in such torment.

That was the first pain that they inflicted on him, and after he had recovered, they took him to a place where he saw more misery. Men and women crying out, "Alas!" and "Welaway!" lay there, faces upward, as the others had lain with faces downward, with feet and hands and heads nailed fast to the earth with nails glowing red. Owain saw loathsome fiery dragons sitting upon them; on others sat black toads, newts, adders, and snakes that ate them, backs and sides. This is the punishment of gluttony; for the love of God be warned, since that sin flourishes all too widely. Owain thought a wind blew among them so bitter and so cold that it overthrew all who lay in purgatory. The fiends quickly leaped upon the sufferers and tore them furiously with their hooks. Whosoever, man or woman, is guilty of impurity in this life, shall suffer in that prison. The fiend said to the knight, "Thou hast been unclean and a great glutton, also; into this torment thou shalt be thrust unless thou wilt return speedily the way thou didst come." Owain said, "Nay, Satan, further still shall I go, through the grace of God Almighty." The fiends would have seized him, but he called upon God Omnipotent, and they lost all their power.

They then led him into a spot where men never did any good deeds, but only shameful and villainous ones. In the fourth field this was, full of torments. There were people hanging by the feet from burning iron hooks, others hung by the neck, the stomach, the back, and in other ways too numerous to mention. Some were hanging by the tongue, and their constant cry was "Alas!" and no other prayer. In a furnace with molten lead and burning brimstone boiling over the fire were many folk. Some lying on gridirons glowing against the flames were people whom Owain had once known, but who were now entirely changed through the penance they suffered. A wild fire surged among them, and all whom it seized, it burned, ten thousand souls and more. Those that hung by feet and neck were thieves, or the companions of thieves, and wrought men woe. Those that hung by the tongue and ever sang "Alas!" and cried so loudly were backbiters in their lives. Beware, man or wife, if thou art fond of chiding! All the places the knight came by were full of the pains of purgatory. Whosoever takes the name of God in vain, or bears any false witness, suffers strong pains there.

Owain saw where a grisly-looking wheel turned; huge it was, burning like a brand as it wound around, and covered with hooks. A hundred thousand souls and more were hanging from the wheel. The fiends turned it about so fast that Sir Owain could not recognize anybody there. Out of the earth came a burning blue fire; it smelled foully, and it went around the wheel, burning the souls to a very fine powder. The wheel that runs thus is for the punishment of covetousness that now reigns everywhere. The covetous man has never enough gold or silver or even ploughs until Death fells him. The fiends said to the knight, "Thou hast been covetous of winning land and men; upon this wheel thou shalt be placed unless thou wilt return at once to thine own country." When he refused, the fiends seized him, bound him fast upon the revolving wheel, and cast him in the midst. When the hooks tore him and the fire burned him, he thought of Jesus Christ. An angel bore him from the wheel, and all the fiends there could do him no harm.

Further he was led in great pain, until they came to a mountain that was red as blood. Men and women stood on it, in misery, it seemed, for they cried as if they were mad. The fiends then said to the knight, "Thou art wondering about these men who make such doleful cheer. They have deserved the wrath of God; soon they shall have such a drink as they will not think pleasant." No sooner had he spoken than there came a blast of wind that took fiends and souls and knight up almost into the firmament, and then cast them down into a foul-smelling river that ran under the mountain of fire as an arrow from a cross-bow. It was as cold as ice, and no one can describe the pain that he suffered. Owain was almost drowned in the water, and became so frenzied and faint that he was well-nigh lost. As soon as he could think upon God he was brought out of the water and carried to land. That pain is the punishment of wrath and envy. Envy was the blast of wind which cast him into the smelling water. Let every man beware of it.

They led him forth quickly until they came to a hall whose like he had never seen before; out of the hall came such heat that the knight began to sweat. He saw so foul a smoke that he stopped, and when the fiends perceived it they were pleased. "Turn again," they began to cry, "thou shalt die, unless thou dost withdraw." When he came to the hall door he saw misery, a half of which he had never imagined. The hall was a place of torments; those folk who were in that prison were stripped of all happiness, for the floor of the hall was full of pits, round and filled to the top with brimstone, brass, copper, and other metals all molten. Men and women stood in these, screaming and crying as if they were mad; some stood up to the waist, others to the breast, and some to the chin. Each man according to his guilt was fixed in that torment, to suffer that great heat. Some bore around their necks bags full of pennies glowing with fire, and such meat they ate. These were usurers in this life. Beware, men and women, lest such sin hinder you. And many souls there walked upright, bearing false measures and false weights, which fiends sat upon. The fiends said to the knight, "Thou must bathe in this lead before thou go hence; because of thy usury and thy sin, thou must wash thyself somewhat." Owain feared that torment, and called upon God Omnipotent and His mother Mary. He was borne out of the hall, from the pains and all the fiends, when he made that outcry.

Soon he was frightened by seeing a flame of fire, mighty and thick, spring out of the earth, like coal and pitch. Of seven colors was this fire, and some of the souls burning in it were yellow, some green, some black, some blue, and some like adders. They were woful indeed. The fiends took the knight to the pit, and said, "Now, Owain, thou mayst find solace, for thou shalt shake with our fellows in the pit of hell. These are our birds in our cage, and this is our court and our castle tower. Dost thou think, Sir Knight, that to those who are brought here anything is sharp? Now turn again, ere it be too late, before we thrust thee into hell gate, for thou shalt never issue out of it by means of any crying or calling upon Mary, or by any other trick." The knight was firm, so the fiends seized and bound him, and cast him far down into that dark, evil, reeking prison. The farther down they thrust him the hotter it was, and he suffered cruelly. With good will and steadfast heart he called upon God Omnipotent to help him out of that torment, and he was borne up out of the pit, otherwise he would have been lost until the day of his death. That suffering, which lasts forever, is for the foul sin of pride.

Outside the pit he realized how God had rescued him. His clothes were torn to pieces, his body was burned all over, and he knew not which way to go. He changed color when he saw more fiends, none of whom he recognized in that strange place. Some of them had sixty eyes that were loathsome and grisly, some had sixty hands. They said, "Thou shalt not be alone, but shalt have us for company, to teach thee the new laws, as before thou didst learn them in that spot where thou wast among our fellows." The fiends then led the knight towards a foul-smelling body of water, such as he had never seen. It was many miles in breadth and black as pitch. Owain saw passing over it a very strong but narrow bridge. The fiends said, "Lo, Sir Knight, seest thou this? This is the bridge of paradise; across this thou must go, and we shall hurl stones at thee, and the wind shall blow thee over and work thee woe. Thou wilt never pass over this without falling into the midst of our fellows to dwell forevermore. When thou hast fallen down, then all our company will come and wound thee with their hooks. We shall teach thee a new sport, for thou hast served us many a day, and we will lead thee into hell."

Owain beheld the bridge and the water under it, so black and dreadful, and began to be sore afraid because of one thing he noted: never did motes dance in the sunbeam thicker than that company of fiends. The bridge[28] was as high as a tower and as sharp as a razor; narrow it was, and the water running underneath burned with lightning and thunder. He was exceedingly woful. There is no clerk who may write with ink, nor no man who can think, nor no master who can divine, one half of the torment there is under the bridge of paradise. We are told that there is the true entrance to hell. Saint Paul bears witness. Whosoever falls down from the bridge will never have redemption in any degree.

The fiends then said to the knight, "There is no need for thee to cross this bridge. Flee pain, sorrow, and woe, and we will lead thee fairly back to that place from which thou didst come." Owain began to recall from how many of the tricks of the fiends God had saved him, so he set his foot upon the bridge, and felt no sharp edge, nor was he at all afraid. When the fiends saw that he was more than half over, they began to cry aloud, "Alas, alas, that he was born, this knight we have lost from our prison!"

When he was safely across the bridge, he thanked God Omnipotent and His mother Mary, who had sent him such grace, that he was delivered out of torment into a better region. A cloth of gold was brought to him, he knew not how except that God sent it. That cloth he put on, and at once all his wounds from being burned were whole, and he thanked the Trinity. Looking ahead, he saw what seemed to be a stone wall. He gazed far and near, but could see no end of this, which shone all of red gold. Farther on he saw a gate, a fairer one may never be in this world. It was made, not of wood nor of steel, but of red gold and of precious stones, created by God out of nothing. Jasper, topaz, crystal, pearls, and coral, rich sapphires, rubies, chalcedonies, onyxes, and diamonds were wrought into tabernacles. Richer they might not be; they had pillars small and beautifully fashioned, with arches of carbuncles, knots of red gold, and pinnacles of crystal. Inasmuch as our Savior is more skilful than any goldsmith or painter in any land, so are the gates of paradise more richly wrought than any other.

The gates unfastened themselves, and a fragrance like balm came forth, of such sweetness that the knight took fresh strength and thought that now he would be a thousand times better prepared to suffer pain and woe and to fight against all the fiends if he had to go back the way he came. He went near the gate and saw approaching a procession of folk with gracious countenances, bearing tapers and candlesticks of gold and crosses and banners. Popes there were, of great dignity, and many cardinals, kings and queens, knights, abbots superior, monks, canons, and preaching friars, and bishops who bore crosses. Minorite friars and Jacobins, Carmelites and Austin friars, black and white nuns—all manner of religious orders went in that procession. The order of wedlock came also, with many men and women who thanked God for sending his grace to deliver the knight from torment by the fiends, and to bring him alive to that spot. When the praises had thus been sung, two archbishops came out of the midst of that company, bearing palms of gold. They advanced to the knight, and, taking him between them, led him up and down, and showed him still greater joys and also much melody. Merry were their carols of joy and minstrelsy. They went carolling with a joy no man can divine, singing and praising God; angels guided them with harps and fiddles and psaltery, and bells rang merrily. No man may carol there except him who is clean from sin and who has given up all folly. Now may God and His mother Mary, in memory of Thy wounds, grant that we may carol in that hall. This same joy is granted for love and charity towards God and all mankind. Whosoever lets earthly love alone and loves God in Trinity may carol thus.

Other joys he saw in abundance: high trees, with many branches, on which the birds of heaven sat and sang their notes with merry glee, some low, some intermediate, and some high. He thought indeed that with the song of those birds he might live happily there until the end of the world. Then he saw the tree of life, because of which Adam and his wife went to hell. Fair were the arbors, there, with flowers,—roses and lilies of many colors, primroses and periwinkle, mint, featherfoy and eglantine, columbine, and many others, more than man can think. Herbs of other kinds than on earth grow there, though that is the least of the praises of the place. Forever they spring up green, sweeter than licorice, unchanging in winter and summer.

There are wells in that spot, with water sweeter than any mead, and out of the chief one which Owain saw, run the four streams of paradise. Pison, they call one stream that gleams brightly, because men find gold there; Gihon is another that is much praised for the precious stones in its bed; the third stream is named Euphrates, it runs straight along; and the fourth is Tigris, in all the world is there none other with stones so bright. Whosoever loves to live in purity shall have that same bliss and see that same sight. More Owain saw there, under God's glory on high; blessed be His might!

Some souls he saw apart by themselves, and some in groups of ten or twelve; and when they met together they made as much rejoicing as sister does with brother. Some he saw going about in scarlet red, some in purple well wrought, and others in thin silk. They wore tunics and albs, like what the priest wears at mass, some covered with gold work. The knight knew well by their clothing in what state they were, and what deeds they had done when they were men's companions. I will tell you a fair similitude drawn from the clear stars; inasmuch as one star is brighter to the sight and of more power than three others, so is it with the joys of paradise. They are not all alike, yet he who has the least joy thinks he has the most of all and calls himself very rich.

The bishops came again and, taking him between them, led him up and down and said, "Brother, God be praised, thy wish is fulfilled. Now listen to our counsel. Thou hast seen with thine eyes both the joys and the pains. We will tell thee ere thou dost pass hence, of our common fate. That land that is so full of sorrow, evening and morning, where thou as well as many other souls didst suffer sorely, is called by men purgatory. And this land, where thou now art, so wide and spacious and so full of bliss, is called paradise. No man may come here until he has been purged and made clean there. When they come hither, we lead them into joy, sometimes by groups of twelve and ten. And some are so bound, that they know not how long they must endure the heat; but if their friends who are left on earth have masses sung, or else give food or some other kind of alms, all the better will these folk speed and will come out of their misery into this paradise, where joy and bliss ever are, and will live here in perfect peace. Just as they come out of purgatory, so pass we on to God's glory, which is the high kingdom of the celestial paradise, wherein enter only Christian folk to a joy unequalled. When we come out of the fire of purgatory we cannot pass at once into that place nor see God's face, but must dwell here a long time. Even the child born tonight must pass through that pain before he can enter heaven, and how much harder is it for an old man who has been long in sin to come hither!"

Forth they went until they saw a very high mountain where all was pleasure. Finally they came to the top, and saw all its joys. There were all manner of bird songs; much delight was there and evermore shall be. There is more joy in a bird's mouth than in any harp or fiddle or crouth,[29] whether on land or sea. That land so fair is called the terrestrial paradise; the other paradise, which is the kingdom of God, is above the air and has joys unequalled. (In the earthly paradise Owain was, which Adam had lost, and if Adam had done according to the will of God, neither he nor his offspring would have had to depart out of that joy. Yet, since Adam broke God's commandment so soon, God made him delve with pick and spade in the earth, to help his wife and himself. God was very wroth with him. An angel of stern countenance, bearing a sword of fire, came and made them sore afraid, and drove them out into the world, where they lived evermore in sorrow and woe. And when he died he came to hell, as did all his descendants, until the Son of God was born, by whose passion and death man was brought out of that prison.)[30]

The bishops commanded the knight to tell them whether heaven seemed white or gray, blue or red, yellow or green. The knight answered, "Methinks it is a thousand times brighter than any gold." "Yet," said the bishop, "that very place which is so bright is only the entrance, and every day, to make us blithe, we are refreshed by a sweet fragrance, which is food to our soul."

Anon the knight was aware that a flame of fire issued out from heaven's gate, and he thought that it flew all over paradise, giving forth a sweet smell. The Holy Ghost, in form of fire, alighted then upon the knight, by whose virtue he lost all his earthliness; and for this he thanked God's grace.

Then the bishop said, "God feeds us each day with His bread, but we have no such knowledge of His grace, nor such a vision of His face as have those who are on high. The souls who are at God's feast have joy that lasts without end. Now thou, because of our common fate, must return again the way thou didst come. Keep thyself from mortal sin, so that when thou art dead thou mayst be led by angels into the joy that has no end."

Then Owain wept bitterly and prayed for God's mercy that he might dwell there and might not behold again the strong pains of hell. From his prayer he got no gain; so he took his leave and departed, although he was very sorrowful. Fiends he saw—ten thousand flying from him fast as arrows from a cross-bow. When he came to the hall he found the thirteen men therein. They all held up their hands, and thanked the mercy of Jesus Christ a thousand times and more, and bade Owain not to rest until he had returned to Ireland as quickly as he could go. And, as I find in the story, the prior of the purgatory had a token that night that Owain had overcome his woes and would appear on the morrow, through grace of God Almighty.

Then the prior, at the head of a procession with cross and banner, went at once to the hole where Owain had gone, and soon they saw a gleam of light like a bright fire burning; then in the midst of the light came Owain, the knight of God. Then they knew well that Owain had been in paradise and in purgatory, and that he was a holy man. They led him into holy church, to do God's office and to say his prayers. On the fifteenth day, the knight took staff and scrip and sought the holy place where Christ bought us so dearly upon the cross and where He rose from death to life through the virtue of His five wounds. Blessed may He be! And Bethlehem, too, he visited, where Christ was born of Mary, His mother like the flower of the thorn. At last, returning to Ireland, Owain took the monk's habit and lived there seven years. When he died he entered, truly, into the high joys of paradise, through the help of God's grace. Now for the love of Saint Owain, may God grant us the bliss of heaven above, in the presence of His sweet face! Amen!

Translated by M. H. S.

SAINTS' LIVES

THE LIFE OF SAINT BRANDON[31]

Saint Brandon, the holy man, was a monk and born in Ireland, and there he was abbot of a house wherein were a thousand monks, and there he had a full strait and holy life in great penance and abstinence, and he governed his monks full virtuously. And then within short while after there came to him an holy abbot, that hight Birinus, to visit him, and each of them was joyful of other. And then Saint Brandon began to tell to the Abbot Birinus of many wonders that he had seen in divers lands, and when Birinus heard that of Saint Brandon, he began to sigh and sore weep, and Saint Brandon comforted him in the best wise that he could, saying, "Ye come hither for to be joyful with me, and therefore for God's love leave your mourning, and tell me what marvels ye have seen in the great sea ocean that compasseth all the world about and all other waters come out of him, which runneth in all parts of the earth."

And then Birinus began to tell to Saint Brandon and to his monks the marvels that he had seen, full sore weeping, and said: "I have a son, his name is Mervok, and he was a monk of great fame, which had great desire to seek about by ship in divers countries to find a solitary place wherein he might dwell secretly out of the business of the world for to serve God quietly with more devotion. And I counselled him to sail into an island far in the sea beside the Mountain of Stones, which is full well known; and then he made him ready and sailed thither with his monks. And when he came thither he liked the place full well, where he and his monks served our Lord full devoutly."

And then Birinus saw in a vision that this monk Mervok was sailed right far eastward in the sea, more than three days' sailing, and suddenly, to his seeming, there came a dark cloud and over-covered them, that a great part of the day they saw no light, and, as our Lord would, the cloud passed away and they saw a full fair island, and thitherward they drew. In that island was joy and mirth enough, and the earth of that island shined as bright as the sun; and there were the fairest trees and herbs that ever any man saw, and there were many precious stones shining bright, and every herb there was full of flowers, and every tree full of fruit, so that it was a glorious sight and a heavenly joy to abide there.

And then there came to them a fair young man, and full courteously he welcomed them all, and called every monk by his name, and he said that they were much bound to praise the name of our Lord Jesu, that would, of His grace, shew to them this glorious place where is ever day and never night. And this place is called Paradise Terrestrial. By this island is another island wherein no man may come, and this young man said to them: "Ye have been here half a year without meat, drink, or sleep," and they supposed they had not been there the space of half an hour, so merry and joyful they were there. And the young man told them that this is the place that Adam and Eve dwelt in first, and ever should have dwelled here if that they had not broken the commandment of God.

Then the young man brought them to their ship again and said they might no longer abide there; and when they were all shipped, suddenly this young man vanished away out of their sight. And then within short time after, by the purveyance of our Lord Jesu Christ, they came to the abbey where Saint Brandon dwelled, and then he with his brethren received them goodly and demanded them where they had been so long, and they said: "We have been in the Land of Behest, tofore the gates of paradise, whereas is ever day and never night." And they said all that the place is full delectable, for yet all their clothes smelled of the sweet and joyful place.

And then Saint Brandon purposed soon after for to seek that place by God's help, and anon began to purvey for a good ship and a strong, and victualled it for seven years. And then he took his leave of all his brethren and took twelve monks with him, but, ere they entered into the ship, they fasted forty days and lived devoutly, and each of them received the sacrament. And when Saint Brandon with his twelve monks were entered into the ship, there came other two of his monks and prayed him that they might sail with him, and then he said: "Ye may sail with me, but one of you shall go to hell ere you come again." But for all that they would go with him.

And then Saint Brandon bade the shipmen to wind up the sail, and forth they sailed in God's name, so that on the morrow they were out of sight of any land. And forty days and forty nights after they sailed plat east, and then they saw an island far from them; and they sailed thitherward as fast as they could, and they saw a great rock of stone appear above all the water; and three days they sailed about it ere they could get into the place, but at the last, by the purveyance of God, they found a little haven and there went aland every each one. And then suddenly came a fair hound, and fell down at the feet of Saint Brandon and made him good cheer in his manner. And then he bade his brethren be of good cheer, "For our Lord hath sent to us his messenger to lead us into some good place." And the hound brought them into a fair hall, where they found the tables spread, ready set full of good meat and drink. And then Saint Brandon said graces, and then he and his brethren sat down and ate and drank of such as they found, and there were beds ready for them wherein they took their rest after their long labour.

And on the morn they returned again to their ship, and sailed a long time in the sea after, ere they could find any land, till at last, by the purveyance of God, they saw far from them a full fair island, full of green pasture, wherein were the whitest and greatest sheep that ever they saw; for every sheep was as great as an ox. And soon after came to them a goodly old man, which welcomed them and made to them good cheer, and said: "This is the Island of Sheep. And here is never cold weather but ever summer, and that causeth the sheep to be so great and white: they eat of the best grass and herbs that is anywhere." And then this old man took his leave of them and bade them sail forth right east, and within short time, by God's grace, they should come into a place like paradise wherein they should keep their Eastertide.

And then they sailed forth, and came soon after to that land, but could find no haven because of little depth in some place, and in some place were great rocks. But at the last they went upon an island, weening to them that they had been safe, and made thereon a fire for to dress their dinner, but Saint Brandon abode still in the ship. When the fire was right hot and the meat nigh sodden, then this island began to move, whereof the monks were afeard, and fled anon to the ship and left the fire and meat behind them, and marvelled sore of the moving. And Saint Brandon comforted them and said that it was a great fish named Jasconye, which laboureth night and day to put his tail in his mouth but for greatness he may not.

And then anon they sailed west three days and three nights ere they saw any land, wherefore they were right heavy, but soon after, as God would, they saw a fair island full of flowers, herbs, and trees; whereof they thanked God of His good grace, and anon they went on land. And when they had gone long in this, they found a full fair well, and thereby stood a fair tree full of boughs, and on every bough sat a fair bird, and they sat so thick on the tree that unnethe any leaf of the tree might be seen. The number of them was so great and they sang so merrily that it was an heavenly noise to hear, wherefore Saint Brandon kneeled down on his knees and wept for joy, and made his prayers devoutly to our Lord God to know what these birds meant. And then anon one of these birds fled from the tree to Saint Brandon, and he with flickering of his wings made a full merry noise like a fiddle, that him seemed he heard never so joyful a melody. And then Saint Brandon commanded the bird to tell him the cause why they sat so thick on the tree and sang so merrily. And then the bird said: "Sometime we were angels in heaven. But when our master Lucifer fell down into hell for his high pride, we fell with him for our offences, some higher and some lower, after the quality of the trespass, and because our trespass is but little, therefore our Lord hath set us here, out of all pain, in full great joy and mirth, after His pleasing, here to serve Him in this tree in the best manner we can. The Sunday is a day of rest from all worldly occupation, and therefore this day all we be made as white as any snow for to praise our Lord in the best wise we may." And then this bird said to Saint Brandon: "It is twelve months passed that ye departed from your abbey, and in the seventh year hereafter ye shall see the place that ye desire to come to. And all these seven years, ye shall keep your Easter here with us every year, and in the end of the seventh year ye shall come unto the Land of Behest."

And this was on Easter Day that the bird said these words to Saint Brandon; and then this fowl flew again to his fellows that sat on the tree, and then the birds began to sing evensong so merrily that it was an heavenly noise to hear. And after supper Saint Brandon and his fellows went to bed and slept well; and on the morn they arose betimes, and then those birds began matins, prime, and hours, and all such service as Christian men use to sing. And Saint Brandon with his fellows abode there eight weeks, till Trinity Sunday was passed.

And they sailed again to the Island of Sheep, and they victualled them well, and took their leave of that old man and returned again to ship. And then the bird of the tree came again to Saint Brandon and said: "I am come to tell you that ye shall sail from hence into an island, wherein is an abbey of twenty-four monks, which is from this place many a mile, and there ye shall hold your Christmas and your Easter with us, like as I told you." And then this bird flew to his fellows again.

Then Saint Brandon and his fellows sailed forth in the ocean, and soon after fell a great tempest on them in which they were greatly troubled long time and sore for-laboured. And after that they found, by the purveyance of God, an island that was far from them, and then they full meekly prayed our Lord to send them thither in safety, but it was forty days after ere they came thither; wherefore all the monks were so weary of that trouble that they set little price by their lives, and cried continually to our Lord to have mercy on them, and bring them to that island in safety. And, by the purveyance of God, they came at the last into a little haven, but it was so strait that unnethe[32] the ship might come in; and after, they came to an anchor, and anon the monks went to land. And when they had long walked about, at the last they found two fair wells: one was fair and clear water, but the other was somewhat troubly and thick. And then they thanked our Lord fully humbly that had brought them thither in safety; and they would fain have drunken of that water, but Saint Brandon charged them they should not take without licence: "For if we abstain us awhile, our Lord will purvey for us in the best wise." And anon after came to them a fair old man with hoar hair, and welcomed them full meekly and kissed Saint Brandon, and led them by many a fair well till they came to a fair abbey, where they were received with great honour and solemn procession with twenty-four monks all in royal copes of cloth of gold, and a royal cross was before them. And then the abbot welcomed Saint Brandon and his fellowship, and kissed them full meekly, and took Saint Brandon by the hand and led him with his monks into a fair hall, and set them down arow upon the bench, and the abbot of the place washed all their feet with fair water of the well that they saw before, and after, he led them into a fraitour[33] and there set them among his convent. And anon there came one, by the purveyance of God, which served them well of meat and drink, for every monk had set before him a fair white loaf and white roots and herbs which were right delicious, but they wist not what roots they were. And they drank of the water of the fair clear well which they saw before when they came first aland, which Saint Brandon forbade them.

And then the abbot came and cheered Saint Brandon and his monks and bade them eat and drink for charity: "For every day our Lord sendeth a goodly old man that covereth this table and setteth our meat and drink tofore us, but we know not how it cometh, ne we ordain never no meat ne drink for us, and yet we have been eighty years here, and ever our Lord, worshipped may He be, feedeth us. We be twenty-four monks in number, and every ferial[34] day of the week He sendeth to us twelve loaves, and every Sunday and feast day twenty-four loaves, and the bread that we leave at dinner we eat at supper. And now at your coming our Lord hath sent unto us forty-eight loaves, for to make you and us merry together as brethren. And always twelve of us go to dinner while other twelve keep the quire, and thus have we done these eighty years, for so long have we dwelled in this abbey. We came hither out of the abbey of Saint Patrick in Ireland, and thus as ye see our Lord hath purveyed for us, but none of us knoweth how it cometh but God alone to whom be given honour and laud, world without end. Here in this land is ever fair weather, and none of us hath ever been sick sith we came hither. And when we go to mass or to any other service of our Lord in the church, anon seven tapers of wax be set in the quire and be lighted at every time without man's hand, and so burn day and night at every hour of service, and never waste ne minish as long as we have been here, which is eighty years."

Then Saint Brandon went to the church with the abbot of the place, and there they said evensong together full devoutly, and then Saint Brandon looked upward towards the crucifix and saw our Lord hanging on the cross, which was made of fine crystal and curiously wrought. And in the quire were twenty-four seats for twenty-four monks, and the seven tapers burning, and the abbot's seat was made in the midst of the quire. Then Saint Brandon demanded of the abbot how long they had kept that silence, that none of them spake to other, and he said: "This twenty-four years we spake never one to another." And then Saint Brandon wept for joy of their holy conversation. And then Saint Brandon desired of the abbot that he and his monks might dwell there still with him. To whom the abbot said: "Sir, that may ye not do in no wise, for our Lord hath shewed to you in what manner ye shall be guided till the seven years be fulfilled, and after that term thou shalt with thy monks return into Ireland in safety, but one of the two monks that came last to you shall dwell in the Island of Ankers,[35] and that other shall go quick to hell."

And as Saint Brandon kneeled in the church, he saw a bright shining angel come in at the window, and lighted all the lights in the church, and then he flew out again at the window unto heaven. Then Saint Brandon marvelled greatly how the light burned so fair and wasted not. Then the abbot said, "It is written that Moses saw a bush all on afire and yet it burned not, and therefore marvel not hereof, for the might of our Lord is now as great as it ever was."

And when Saint Brandon had dwelled there from Christmas even till the twelfth day was passed, then he took his leave of the abbot of the convent and returned with his monks to his ship. And he sailed from thence with his monks toward the abbey of Saint Illaries; but they had great tempests in the sea from that time till Palm Sunday.

And then they came to the Island of Sheep and there were received of the old man, which brought them to a fair hall and served them. And on Shere Thursday[36] after supper he did wash all their feet and kissed them, like as our Lord did to His disciples, and there they abode till Saturday, Easter Even; and they departed and sailed to the place where the fish lay; and anon they saw their cauldron upon the fish's back, which they had left there twelve months tofore. There they kept the service of the resurrection, on the fish's back, and after, they sailed that same day by the morning to the island whereas the tree of birds was, and then the said bird welcomed Saint Brandon and all his fellowship, and went again to the tree and sang full merrily. And there he and his monks dwelled from Easter till Trinity Sunday, as they did the year before, in full great joy and mirth. And daily they heard the merry service of the birds sitting on the tree.

And then the bird told to Saint Brandon that he should return again at Christmas to the abbey of monks, and at Easter thither again, and the other deal of the year labour in the ocean in full great perils, and from year to year till the seven years be accomplished. "And then shall ye come to the joyful place of paradise and dwell there forty days in full great joy and mirth. And after, ye shall return home into your own abbey in safety, and there end your life and come to the bliss of heaven to which our Lord bought you with His precious blood."

And then the angel of our Lord ordained all thing that was needful to Saint Brandon and to his monks in victuals and all other things necessary, and then they thanked our Lord of His great goodness He had shewed to them oft in their great need, and sailed forth in the great sea ocean, abiding the mercy of our Lord in great trouble and tempests.

And soon after came to them an horrible fish which followed the ship long time, casting so much water out of his mouth into the ship that they supposed to have been drowned, wherefore they devoutly prayed God to deliver them of that great peril. And anon after, came another fish, greater than he, out of the west sea, and fought with him, and at the last clave him into three pieces, and then returned again. And then they thanked meekly our Lord for their deliverance from this great peril, but they were in great heaviness because their victuals were nigh spent. But, by the ordinance of our Lord, there came a bird and brought to them a great branch of a vine full of red grapes, by which they lived fourteen days, and then they came to a little island, wherein were many vines full of grapes. And they there landed and thanked God, and gathered as many grapes as they lived by forty days after, alway sailing in the sea in many storms and tempests.

And as they thus sailed, suddenly came flying towards them a great grip[37] which assailed them and was like to have destroyed them. Wherefore they devoutly prayed for help and aid of our Lord Jesu Christ. And then the bird of the tree of the island where they had holden their Easter tofore came to the grip and smote out both his eyes and after slew him, whereof they thanked our Lord.

And then they sailed forth continually till Saint Peter's day, and then sang they solemnly their service in the honour of the feast. And in that place the water was so clear that they might see all the fishes that were about them, whereof they were full sore aghast, and the monks counselled Saint Brandon to sing no more, for all the fishes lay then as they had slept. And then Saint Brandon said: "Dread ye not, for ye have kept by two Easters the feast of the resurrection upon the great fish's back, and therefore dread ye not of these little fishes." And then Saint Brandon made him ready and went to mass and bade his monks to sing the best way they could, and then anon all the fishes awoke and came about the ship so thick that unnethe they might see the water for the fishes, and when the mass was done, all the fishes departed so as they were no more seen. And seven days they sailed always in that clear water.

And then there came a south wind and drove the ship northward, whereas they saw an island full dark and full of stench and smoke, and there they heard great blowing and blasting of bellows, but they might see nothing, but heard great thundering, whereof they were sore afraid and blessed them oft. And soon after, there came one starting out all burning in fire and gazed full ghastly on them with great staring eyes, of whom the monks were aghast, and at his departing from them he made the horriblest cry that might be heard. And soon there came a great number of fiends and assailed them with hooks and burning iron malles, which ran on the water, following their ship fast, in such wise that it seemed all the sea to be on fire. But by the pleasure of our Lord, they had no power to hurt nor grieve them nor their ship: wherefore the fiends began to roar and cry and threw their hooks and malles at them. And they then were sore afeard and prayed to God for comfort and help, for they saw the fiends all about the ship, and them seemed then all the island and the sea to be on fire. And with a sorrowful cry all the fiends departed from them and returned to the place that they came from. And then Saint Brandon told to them that this was a part of hell, and therefore he charged them to be steadfast in the faith, for they should yet see many a dreadful place ere they came home again.

And then came the south wind and drove them further to the north, where they saw an hill all of fire, and a foul smoke and stench coming from thence, and the fire stood on each side of the hill, like a wall, all burning. And then one of his monks began to cry and weep full sore, and said that his end was come and that he might abide no longer in the ship; and anon he leapt out of the ship into the sea, and then he cried and roared full piteously, cursing the time that he was born and also father and mother that begat him, because they saw no better to his correction in his young age, "for now I must go to perpetual pain." And then the saying of the blessed Saint Brandon was verified that he said to him when he entered. Therefore it is good a man to do penance and forsake sin, for the hour of death is uncertain.

And then anon the wind turned into the north and drove the ship into the south, which sailed seven days continually, and they came to a great rock standing in the sea, and thereon sat a naked man in full great misery and pain, for the waves of the sea had so beaten his body that all the flesh was gone off, and nothing left but sinews and bare bones. And when the waves were gone, there was a canvas that hung over his head which beat his body full sore with the blowing of the wind; and also there were two ox-tongues and a great stone that he sat on which did him full great ease.

And then Saint Brandon charged him to tell him what he was. And he said: "My name is Judas, that sold our Lord Jesu Christ for thirty pence, which sitteth here thus wretchedly, howbeit I am worthy to be in the greatest pain that is. But our Lord is so merciful that He hath rewarded me better than I have deserved, for of right my place is in the burning hell, but I am here but certain times of the year, that is, from Christmas to Twelfth Day, and from Easter till Whitsuntide be past, and every feastful day of our Lady, and every Saturday noon till Sunday that evensong be done. But all other times, I lie still in hell, in full burning fire, with Pilate, Herod, and Caiaphas; therefore accursed be the time that ever I knew them."

And then Judas prayed Saint Brandon to abide still there all that night, and that he would keep him there still, that the fiends should not fetch him to hell. And Saint Brandon said, "With God's help thou shalt abide here all this night." And then he asked Judas what cloth that was that hung over his head, and he said that it was a cloth that he gave to a leper, which was bought with the money that he stole from our Lord when he bare His purse. "Wherefore, it doth to me full great pain now in beating my face with the blowing of the wind, and these two ox-tongues that hang here above me, I gave them sometime to two priests to pray for me; them I bought with mine own money, and therefore they ease me, because the fishes of the sea gnaw on them and spare me. And this stone that I sit on lay sometime in a desolate place where it eased no man, and I took it thence, and laid it in a foul way, where it did much ease to them that went by that way, and therefore it easeth me now, for every good deed shall be rewarded and every evil deed shall be punished."

And the Sunday, against even, there came a great multitude of fiends, blasting and roaring, and they bade Saint Brandon go thence that they might have their servant Judas, "For we dare not come in the presence of our master but if we bring him to hell with us." And then said Saint Brandon: "I let not you to do your master's commandment, but by the power of the Lord Jesu Christ, I charge you to leave him this night till tomorrow." They said: "How darest thou help him that so sold his master for thirty pence to the Jews, and caused Him also to die the most shameful death upon the cross?" And then Saint Brandon charged the fiends by His passion that they should not noy him that night. And then the fiends went their way, roaring and crying, towards hell to their master the great devil. And then Judas thanked Saint Brandon so ruthfully that it was a pity to see. And on the morrow the fiends came with a horrible noise, saying that they had that night suffered great pain because they brought not Judas, and said that he should suffer double pain the six days following; and they took then Judas, trembling for fear, with them to pain.

And after, Saint Brandon sailed southward three days and three nights, and on the Friday they saw an island, and then Saint Brandon began to sigh, and said: "I see the island wherein Saint Paul the hermit dwelleth and hath dwelled there forty years without meat and drink ordained by man's hand."

And when they came to the land, Saint Paul came and welcomed them humbly. He was old and foregrown[38] so that no man might see his body. Of whom Saint Brandon said, weeping: "I see a man that liveth more like an angel than a man, wherefore we monks may be ashamed that we live not better." Then Saint Paul said to Saint Brandon: "Thou art better than I, for our Lord hath shewed to thee more privities than he hath done to me; wherefore, thou oughtest to be more praised than I."

To whom Saint Paul said: "Some time I was a monk of Saint Patrick's abbey in Ireland and was warden of the place whereas men enter into Saint Patrick's Purgatory, and on a day there came one to me and I asked him what he was, and he said: 'I am your abbot, Patrick, and charge thee that thou depart from hence tomorn early to the sea-side, and there thou shalt find a ship into which thou must enter, which God has ordained for thee, whose will thou must accomplish.' And so the next day I arose and went forth, and found the ship, in which I entered, and, by the purveyance of God, was I brought into this island the seventh day after. And then I left the ship and went to land, and there I walked up and down a good while, and then, by the purveyance of God, there came an otter, going upon his hinder feet, and brought me a flint stone and an iron to smite fire with, in the two foreclaws of his feet, and also, he had about his neck great plenty of fish, which he cast down before me and went his way. And I smote fire, and made a fire of sticks, and did seethe the fish, by which I lived three days. And then the otter came again and brought me fish for other three days, and thus he hath done this fifty-one years, through the grace of God. And there was a great stone out of which our blessed Lord made to spring fair water clear and sweet, whereof I drink daily. And thus have I lived one and fifty years. I was forty years old when I came hither, and am now an hundred and eleven years old, and abide till it please our Lord Jesu Christ to send for me; and if it pleased Him, I would fain be discharged of this wretched life."

And then he bade Saint Brandon to take of the water of the well and to carry it into his ship, "for it is time that thou depart, for thou hast a great journey to do, for thou shalt sail to an island which is forty days' sailing hence, where thou shalt hold thine Easter like as thou hast done tofore, whereas the tree of birds is. And from thence thou shalt sail into the Land of Behest, and shalt abide there forty days, and after return home into thy country in safety."

And then these holy men took leave each of other, and they wept both full sore, and kissed each other. Then Saint Brandon entered into the ship, and sailed forty days even south, in full great tempest, and on Easter Even they came to their procurator, which made to them good cheer, as he had beforetime. And from thence they came to the great fish whereon they said matins and mass on Easter Day, and when the mass was done, the fish began to move and swam forth fast into the sea, whereof the monks were sore aghast which stood upon him, for it was a great marvel to see such a fish, so great as all a country, for to swim so fast in the water, but, by the will of our Lord, this fish set all the monks aland in the Paradise of Birds, all whole and sound, and then returned to the place he came from. And then Saint Brandon and his monks thanked our Lord of their deliverance of the great fish, and kept their Eastertide till Trinity Sunday, like as they had done beforetime.

And after this they took their ship and sailed east forty days, and at the forty days' end it began to hail right fast, and therewith came a dark mist which lasted long after, which feared Saint Brandon and his monks, and they prayed to our Lord to keep and help them. And then anon came their procurator and bade them to be of good cheer, for they were come into the Land of Behest.

And soon after, that mist passed away, and anon they saw the fairest country eastward that any man might see, and it was so clear and bright that it was a heavenly sight to behold, and all the trees were charged with ripe fruit, and herb full of flowers. In which land they walked forty days, but they could not see none end of that land, and there was always day and never night, and the land temperate, ne too hot ne too cold.

And at the last they came to a fair river, but they durst not go over, and there came to them a fair young man, and welcomed them courteously and called each by name, and did great reverence to Saint Brandon. And he said to them: "Be ye now joyful, for this is the land that ye have sought, but our Lord will that ye depart hence hastily, and He will show you more of His secrets, when ye come again into the sea, and our Lord will that ye lade your ship with the fruit of this land, and hie you hence, for ye may no longer abide here, but thou shalt sail again to thine own country, and soon after thou comest home thou shalt die. And this water that thou seest here departeth the world asunder, for on that other side of this water may no man come that is in this life. And the fruit that ye see here is always thus ripe every time of the year; and always it is here light as ye now see. And he that keepeth our Lord's hests at all times shall see this land or he pass out of this world."

And then Saint Brandon and his monks took of that fruit as much as they would, and also took with them great plenty of precious stones, and then took their leave, and went to ship weeping sore because they might no longer abide there. And then they took their ship and came home into Ireland in safety, whom their brethren received with great joy, giving thankings to our Lord, which had kept them all these seven years from many a peril and brought them home in safety, to whom be given honour and glory, world without end. Amen.

And soon after, this holy man, Saint Brandon, waxed feeble and sick and had but little joy of this world, but ever after his joy and mind was in the joys of heaven. And in a short time after, he, being full of virtues, departed out of this life to everlasting life, and was worshipfully buried in a fair abbey, which he himself founded, where our Lord shewed for this holy saint many fair miracles. Wherefore let us devoutly pray to this holy saint that he pray for us to our Lord that He have mercy on us; to whom be given laud and honour and empire, world without end. Amen.

Translated by William Caxton

THE LIFE OF SAINT MARGARET [39]

Here followeth the glorious life and passion of the blessed virgin and martyr Saint Margaret, and first of her name

Margaret is said of a precious gem, or ouche, that is named a margaret. Which gem is white, little, and virtuous. So the blessed Margaret was white by virginity, little by humility, and virtuous by operation of miracles. The virtue of this stone is said to be against effusion of blood, against passion of the heart, and to confortation of the spirit. In like wise the blessed Margaret had virtue against shedding of her blood by constancy, for in her martyrdom she was most constant, and also against the passion of the heart, that is to say, temptation of the devil. For she overcame the devil by victory, and to the confortation of the spirit by doctrine, for by her doctrine she comforted much people, and converted to the faith of Christ. Theoteinus, a learned man, wrote her legend.

The holy Saint Margaret was of the city of Antioch, daughter of Theodosius, patriarch and prince of the idols of paynims. And she was delivered to a nurse for to be kept. And when she came to perfect age she was baptized, wherefore she was in great hate of her father.

On a certain day, when she was fifteen years of age and kept the sheep of her nurse with other maidens, the provost Olybrius passed by the way whereas she was, and considered in her so great beauty and fairness, that anon he burned in her love, and sent his servants and bade them take her and bring her to him. "For if she be free, I shall take her to my wife, and if she be bond, I shall make her my concubine." And when she was presented tofore him he demanded her of her lineage, name, and religion. And she answered that she was of noble lineage, and for her name Margaret, and Christian in religion. To whom the provost said: "The two first things be convenient to thee, that is that thou art noble and art called Margaret, which is a most fair name, but the third appertaineth nothing to thee, that so fair a maid and so noble should have a God crucified." To whom she said: "How knowest thou that Christ was crucified?" He answered: "By the books of Christian men." To whom Margaret said: "O what shame is it to you, when you read the pain of Christ and the glory, and believe one thing and deny another." And she said and affirmed Him to be crucified by His will for our redemption, and now liveth ever in bliss. And then the provost, being wroth, commanded her to be put in prison. And the next day following he commanded that she should be brought to him, and then said to her: "O good maid, have pity on thy beauty, and worship our gods, that thou mayest be well." To whom she said: "I worship Him that maketh the earth to tremble, whom the sea dreadeth and the winds and creatures obey." To whom the provost said: "But if thou consent to me I shall make thy body to be all to-torn." To whom Margaret said: "Christ gave Himself over to the death for me, and I desire gladly to die for Christ." Then the provost commanded her to be hanged in an instrument to torment the people, and to be cruelly first beaten with rods, and with iron combs to rend and draw her flesh to the bones, insomuch that the blood ran about out of her body, like as a stream runneth out of a fresh springing well. They that were there wept, and said: "O Margaret, verily we be sorry for thee, which see thy body so foul, and so cruelly torn and rent. O how thy most beauty hast thou lost for thy incredulity and misbelief! Now believe, and thou shalt live." Then said she to them: "O evil counsellors, depart ye, and go from me; this cruel torment of my flesh is salvation of my soul." Then she said to the provost: "Thou shameless hound and insatiable lion, thou hast power over my flesh, but Christ reserveth my soul." The provost covered his face with his mantle, for he might not see so much effusion of blood, and then commanded that she should be taken down, and to shut her fast in prison, and there was seen a marvellous brightness in the prison, of the keepers.

And whilst she was in prison, she prayed our Lord that the fiend that had fought with her, He would visibly show him unto her. And then appeared a horrible dragon and assailed her, and would have devoured her, but she made the sign of the cross, and anon he vanished away. And in another place it is said that he swallowed her into his belly, she making the sign of the cross. And the belly brake asunder, and so she issued out all whole and sound.

This swallowing and breaking of the belly of the dragon is said that it is apocryphal.

After this the devil appeared to her in likeness of a man for to deceive her. And when she saw him, she went to prayer and after arose, and the fiend came to her, and took her by the hand and said: "It sufficeth to thee that thou hast done, but now cease as to my person." She caught him by the head and threw him to the ground and set her right foot on his neck, saying: "Lie still, thou fiend, under the feet of a woman." The devil then cried: "O blessed Margaret, I am overcome. If a young man had overcome me I had not recked, but alas! I am overcome of a tender virgin; wherefore I make the more sorrow, for thy father and mother have been my good friends." She then constrained him to tell why he came to her, and he answered that he came to her to counsel her for to obey the desire and request of the provost. Then she constrained him to say wherefore he tempted so much and so often Christian people. To whom he answered that naturally he hated virtuous men, and though we be oft put aback from them, yet our desire is much to exclude them from the felicity that they fell from, for we may never obtain ne recover our bliss that we have lost. And she then demanded what he was, and he answered: "I am Veltis, one of them whom Solomon closed in a vessel of brass. And after his death it happed that they of Babylon found this vessel, and supposed to have founden great treasure therein, and brake the vessel; and then a great multitude of us devils flew out and filled full the air alway, awaiting and espying where we may assail rightful men." And when he had said thus, she took off her foot and said to him: "Flee hence, thou wretched fiend." And anon the earth opened, and the fiend sank in. Then she was sure, for when she had overcome the master, she might lightly overcome the minister.

Then the next day following, when all the people was assembled, she was presented tofore the judge. And she, not doing sacrifice to their false gods, was cast into the fire, and her body broiled with burning brands, in such wise that the people marvelled that so tender a maid might suffer so many torments. And after that, they put her in a great vessel full of water, fast bounden, that by changing of the torments, the sorrow and feeling of the pain should be the more. But suddenly the earth trembled, and the air was hideous, and the blessed virgin without any hurt issued out of the water, saying to our Lord: "I beseech thee, my Lord, that this water may be to me the font of baptism to everlasting life." And anon there was heard great thunder, and a dove descended from heaven and set a golden crown on her head. Then five thousand men believed in our Lord, and for Christ's love they all were beheaded by the commandment of the provost Olybrius, that time in Campolymeath, the city of Aurelia.

Then Olybrius, seeing the faith of the holy Margaret immoveable, and also fearing that others should be converted to the Christian faith by her, gave sentence and commanded that she should be beheaded. Then she prayed to one Malchus that should behead her, that she might have space to pray. And that got, she prayed to our Lord, saying: "Father Almighty, I yield to Thee thankings that Thou hast suffered me to come to this glory, beseeching Thee to pardon them that pursue me. And I beseech Thee, good Lord, that of Thy abundant grace, Thou wilt grant unto all them that write my passion, read it, or hear, and to them that remember me, that they may deserve to have plain remission and forgiveness of all their sins. And also, good Lord, if any woman with child, travailing in any place, call on me, that Thou wilt keep her from peril, and that the child may be delivered from her belly without any hurt of his members." And when she had finished her prayer there was a voice heard from heaven, saying that her prayers were heard and granted and that the gates of heaven were open and abode for her, and bade her come into the country of everlasting rest. Then she, thanking our Lord, arose up, and bade the hangman accomplish the commandment of the provost. To whom the hangman said: "God forbid that I should slay thee, virgin of Christ." To whom she said: "If thou do it not thou mayest have no part with me." Then he, being afraid and trembling, smote off her head, and he, falling down at her feet, gave up the ghost.

Then Theoteinus took up the holy body, and bare it into Antioch, and buried it in the house of a noble woman and widow named Sincletia. And thus this blessed and holy virgin, Saint Margaret, suffered death, and received the crown of martyrdom the thirteenth kalends of August, as is founden in her story; and it is read in another place that it was the third ides of July. Of this virgin writeth an holy man and saith: "The holy and blessed Margaret was full of the dread of God, sad, stable, and worshipful in religion, arrayed with compunction, laudable in honesty, and singular in patience, and nothing was found in her contrary to Christian religion; hateful to her father, and beloved of our Lord Jesu Christ." Then let us remember this holy virgin that she pray for us in our needs.

Translated by William Caxton

PIOUS TALES

A MIRACLE OF GOD'S BODY[40]

There was a man beyond the sea, a miner who lived in a city and who sought under the earth for the stones out of which men get silver and gold. He worked and dug in the hill, and a dreadful thing happened to him: a large part of the mine fell down, closing him in. His fellows, who were loyal to him, believed that he was dead, so they took counsel together and went to tell his wife. This woman bewailed her husband sorely (would God there were many such women!). She helped his soul in all ways by giving alms and offerings. She offered for his sake at the altar a pitcher full of wine and a fair loaf, also, every day during a whole twelve months, except on one day. Few such women we find now, who are so kind to their husbands, but this wife with all her power wrought for him both day and night.

It happened at the end of the twelve months that his fellows went to the hill and came to the very place where they had left their companion at work. They began right there and, piercing through, found the man in good estate, alive, without any injury or wound. Each one was filled with amazement, and there was good reason why the men should be in doubt as to how he had lived all that year. Then he told them how he had lived there alone. "I have lived a gracious life through the courtesy of my wife, who every day has sent me wine and bread, except on one day, when I ate nothing."

They led the man in to the town and told the miracle everywhere through the city and through the country. At last it happened that he mentioned the name of the day when he fasted, and his wife said the same thing,—the day she made no offering was Good Friday. Now you may hear how a devout deed of alms will feed a man, and so you may understand that God is always pleased with good offerings.

In spite of this tale, trust not your wives, nor your children, but make your offerings yourselves. So kind a woman as I have told about does not live now, you may be sure. And no clerk who reads this will ever find one of such good deeds. You men who are now present and hear about the sacrament, know that the sacrament on the altar has power over all things, as I have shown to the ignorant but not to the learned, for the clerks know it well. Let us pray our Creator that our Saviour, the Sacrament, will save us body and soul, and grant that we may love Him and be His forever.

Translated by M. H. S.

A MIRACLE OF THE VIRGIN[41]

Lord, Maker of all things, Almighty God in majesty, that ever, without beginning, wert and art and shall be, grant us both strength and opportunity so to serve Thy pleasure that we may, through Thy grace, dwell with Thee for ever and aye!

We ought to bear well in mind those miracles of our Lady which are written in true story, showing how helpful she ever is to mankind. Once upon a time it happened in a city,—hearken well and ye may hear,—when Jews were wont to be together among Christians, Christians dwelt in one half of the city, and the Jews were forced to live in one street. The Christian children had made for themselves a pleasant place in a field, and there a Jew's child often played with them. The child's father took no heed of this and never cast an eye upon him, therefore the child came and went whenever he chose to play. So often did they play together that the Jew's son learned their games and was just like one of the Christian children, loved and welcomed by them.

At one Easter time, which the Christians kept with great solemnity, a beautiful minster had been completed in the midst of the city, and to it the Christian folk went to hear both matins and mass, as, by Christian rule, is usual for both the high and the low. Every one in best array, both husbands and wives, attended. The children followed their fathers, as they were wont, and the Jew's child with right good cheer was happy to go with them. When he was well within the church, he thought he had never been so glad as he was at that seemly sight, such as he had never seen before—both lamps and tapers burning brightly, altars wonderfully ornamented, and beautifully wrought gold images of many good saints.

In a chair sat a comely Queen, all decorated with gold; upon her arm she bore a blissful Babe, in kingly crown as He should be. The child looked long at that Lady and at that blissful Babe, and noted how people told their beads before them, as Christian folk do. The Jew's child felt such pleasure in all the sights he saw and thought them all so sweet, that he was almost ravished with joy. When high mass of the day was done, the priest bade all men kneel down; the Jew's child took heed of this and knelt among the

Christians. Although he was pushed about by the crowd, he was not afraid, and he spared no pains until he too received the sacrament. Of such a child no one took notice. When all things were brought to an end, and every Christian drew towards home, the Jew, seeking his child throughout the town, saw him come from the church. He asked his son where he had been while he had sought him all that day, and the boy told the whole story of what he had done and seen. The father then waxed mad with anger and said at once, "Thou gettest thy reward"; and going to his hot oven that gleamed as does a glowing coal, he cast the child into it, intending to burn him to ashes. With the mouth-stone he sealed the oven, and thought that the truth would not be revealed.

When his mother heard this, in the very place where she stood she fell into a frenzy and for woe became as if mad. Always crying out, she went tearing her hair, in every street in that city, now up, now down, everywhere, and folk wondered about her and felt great pity. The mayor and the bailiffs of the town, when they heard that cry, halted her and made inquiry as to why she cried so wildly and put people in such fear and sorrowed so, especially on Easter Day. As soon as she could cease weeping, this woful mother answered, "Sirs, ye have this city to keep; as lords ye must needs execute law. Alas! alas! I am destroyed, and must have help of you; I pray for a just judgment; my cause I shall prove before you. My husband has burned my child—shut him up in a glowing oven! Go, see, sirs, and I will give you gold enough."

Both mayor and bailiffs, together with the people, went to the Jew's oven, and as soon as they had arrived, the mayor commanded, "Put down the stone." Then every man might easily see how the oven roof, that was round, was in appearance like glowing glass from roof to ground. The child sat there whole and sound, not harmed in hand nor hair, amidst the coals which were all about, just as if he sat in a cool arbor. The child's mother, when she saw that, thought she had never been so glad; into the oven she started towards him, and soon had him out with her. And all the people present there wondered at that strange sight and praised God with good intent, for a miracle is more than man's might. They asked him, with one consent, how it was that he had had no harm among the brands that burned so brightly, and the child answered at once:

"Never in all my life have I had such great happiness as came to me after I was put into the oven. Both brands and coals, in truth, that were beneath my feet, like fair flowers, like special spices, seemed sweet to me. The blissful Queen, that Maiden mild, who sits in church on her throne, with that comely King, her Child, that blissful Babe that she holds on her bosom, shielded me from all harm, from coals and brands that burned so clearly, from all the flames that flowed so wildly, and they could never come near me."

Then men and women, all who were there, both small and great, low and high, praised God heartily for this miracle. The Jewess through her son's word was converted to Christ, anon, and the child and all the Jews accepted the law of Christ. The mayor himself examined the Jew to judge of his trespass, and twelve men were sworn to speak the truth and to give their verdict upon the case. They took counsel together, and came back with one consent. The words of their verdict were, "In that same oven he shall be burned."

Thus is ended this story of the miracle written above. Grant us joy in heaven on high, Lord Jesus, for Thy Mother's love. Amen.

Translated by M. H. S.

THE TRANSLATION OF SAINT THOMAS OF CANTERBURY[42]

The translation of the glorious martyr, Saint Thomas of Canterbury, we shall shortly rehearse unto the laud and praising of Almighty God, then in the fiftieth year after his passion, which was the year of jubilee, that is, of remission. For, of ancient time, the fiftieth year was called the year of the jubilee of pardon and remission, and is yet used among religious men. For when a religious man hath continued in his order fifty years, then he shall be admitted to make his jubilee, and that made, he is pardoned and hath remission of many observances that tofore he was bounden unto. Then in this year of jubilee from his passion, was the solemnity of his translation accomplished, in the time of Honorius, the third pope of that name. The which granted yearly remissions and indulgences so great and large, that tofore in no time of mind hath been seen any popes to have granted and given like. Then let us call to mind that on a Tuesday his translation was accomplished. On the Tuesday happed to him many things. On a Tuesday he was born, on a Tuesday he was exiled, on a Tuesday our Lord appeared to him at Pountney in France, saying: "Thomas, my church shall be glorified in thy blood." On a Tuesday he returned from his exile, and on a Tuesday he suffered martyrdom.

Then how this holy translation was fulfilled now ye shall hear. The reverend father in God, Stephen, Archbishop of Canterbury, Richard, Bishop of Salisbury, Walter, the prior of the same place, with the convent, with spiritual songs and devout hymns, when it was night, went to the sepulchre of this holy martyr, and all that night and day of his translation they persevered in prayers and fastings. And after midnight, four priests, elected and thereto chosen, approaching to his body, took up the holy head with great devotion and reverence, and unto them all offered it for to kiss it. Then the archbishop and all the others made great honour to it, and took all the relics of the precious body, and laid them in a chest, and shut it fast with iron locks, and set it in a place for to be kept unto the day that the translation should be solemnized. The day then of this holy translation being come, there were present a great innumerable multitude of people, as well of rich as of poor. There was Pandulphus, a legate of our holy father the pope, and two archbishops of France, of Rheims and Arles, with many other bishops and abbots, and also King Harry the Third with earls and barons, which king himself took the chest upon his shoulders, and with the other prelates and lords, brought it with great joy and honour in to the place where it is now worshipped, and was laid in a fair and much rich shrine. At whose holy translation were showed, by the merits of this holy martyr, Saint Thomas, many miracles. To blind men was given their sight, to deaf men their hearing, to dumb men their speech, and to dead men was restored life.

Among all others there was a man, because of great devotion that he had to be at this holy translation and visit the holy martyr, which came to the bridge at Brentford by London; and when he was in the middle of the bridge, meeting there one, was cast into the water. This man, not forgetting himself, called Saint Thomas unto his help, and besought him not to suffer his pilgrim to perish, ne to be there drowned. And five times he sank down to the ground, and five times arose above the water, and then he was cast to the dry ground. Then he affirmed that he received no water into his mouth, nor into his ears that did to him grievance nor hurt that he felt, save in his falling he felt in his mouth a little salt water; and added more thereto, saying that, when he sank, a bishop held him up that he might not sink.

This holy translation was done and accomplished the year of our Lord twelve hundred and twenty, in the nones of July, at three o'clock, in the fiftieth year after his passion. For this glorious saint our Lord hath showed many great miracles, as well by his life, as after his death and martyrdom. For a little tofore his death a young man died and was raised again by miracle. And he said that he was led to see the holy order of saints in heaven, and there he saw a seat void, and he asked for whom it was, and it was answered to him that it was kept for the great Bishop of England, Saint

Thomas of Canterbury. There was also a simple priest that daily sang no other mass but of our Lady, whereof he was put to Saint Thomas his ordinary, whom accused, he opposed, and found him full simple of conning, wherefore he suspended him, and inhibited him his mass. Wherefore this priest was full sorry, and prayed humbly to our blessed Lady that he might be restored again to say his mass. And then our blessed Lady appeared to this priest, and bade him go to Saint Thomas, and bid him "by the token that the lady whom thou servest hath sewed his shirt of hair with red silk, which he shall find there as he laid it, that he give thee leave to sing mass, and assoil thee of his suspending and thine inhibiting, and restore thee again to thy service." And when Saint Thomas heard this he was greatly abashed, and went and found like as the priest had said, and then assoiled him to say mass as he did before, commanding him to keep this thing secret as long as he lived.

There was a lady in England that desired greatly to have grey eyes, for she had a conceit that she should be the more beauteous in the sight of the people; and only for that cause she made a vow to visit Saint Thomas upon her bare feet. And when she came thither, and had devoutly made her prayers to have her desire, suddenly she wax stark blind, and then she perceived that she had offended and displeased our Lord in that request, and cried God mercy of that offence, and besought him full meekly to be restored of her sight again. And by the merits of the blessed Saint Thomas she was restored to her sight again, and was glad to have her old eyes, and returned home again, and lived holy to her life's end. Also there was a lord's carver that brought water to him at his table, to whom the lord said: "If thou hast ever stolen anything of mine, I pray God and Saint Thomas that thou have no water in the bason," and suddenly it was all void of the water and dry, and there was he proved a thief.

There was a tame bird kept in a cage, which was learned to speak. And on a time he fled out of the cage and flew into the field; and there came a sparrowhawk and would have taken this bird and pursued after. And the bird, being in great dread, cried: "Saint Thomas! help!" like as he had heard others speak, and the sparrowhawk fell down dead, and the bird escaped harmless.

Also there was a man that Saint Thomas loved much in his days, and he fell in a grievous sickness, wherefore he went to the tomb of Saint Thomas to pray for his health; and anon he had his desire and was all whole. And as he turned homeward, being all whole, then he began to dread lest this health should not be the most profitable for his soul. Then he returned again to the tomb of Saint Thomas, and prayed if his health were not profitable to his soul that his old sickness might come again to him. And it came anon again to him, and endured unto his life's end. And in like wise there was a devout blind man which had his sight restored to him again by the merit of Saint Thomas; but after, he repented him, for he could not be so quiet in his mind as he was before, he had then so much letting by seeing the vanities of the world. Wherefore he prayed to our Lord that by the merits of Saint Thomas he might be blind again to the world as he was before, and anon he had his desire, and lived after full holily to his life's end. Who should tell all the miracles that our blessed Lord hath showed for this holy martyr, it should overmuch endure, for ever sith his passion unto this day, God hath showed continually for him many great miracles. Then let us pray this holy saint to be a special advocate for us wretched sinners unto our Lord God, who bring us unto His everlasting bliss in heaven.

Translated by William Caxton

ALLEGORY

AN EXTRACT FROM "THE CASTLE OF LOVE"[43]

The King had a castle made, after His own device, so that it would never dread the assault of any enemies. He set it on a white rock, thick and high, with good ditches all about, deep and wide. Men can never undermine this castle by any kind of craft, nor can any engine do it harm. The castle is ever full of love and grace for any one who has need of succor. Four towers it has, with fair battlements, and three courts. Heart cannot think nor can tongue tell all the bounty and the beauty of this castle. Seven barbicans are set so securely that no manner of shooting from without can cause harm. The castle is painted on the outside in three colors: a red burning color is above, towards the fair towers; the color of the middle portion is blue softer than indigo; and near the ground is green that never changes hue.

These colors cast such light both far and near that when men behold them it greatly comforts their sight. The castle, within, is ever blanched as white as any driven snow. Four fair streams flow out of a well in the middle of the highest tower and fill the ditches. So fair and so good is the water, that he who drinks of it has great bliss. A throne of ivory there was set in this tower, and seven steps lead upward, with great worship and honor. Never was a throne half so fair seen in this world; nor did prince or queen ever have so beautiful a one. It was made subtilely, by wondrous design, and a rainbow steadfastly arched above it. The King's Son made it for His own seat; never was there one so fair, nor shall there ever be.

This castle of solace and of succor is the blessed body of her who bore our Saviour, and is a refuge for all mankind. Whosoever flees thither shall find succor. The rock, white and fair and stable, is her heart in all its holiness, that made her serve God without fear, in sovereign purity of meekness and maidenhood. The green color, by the ground, that will last so well, is the truth of our lady, aye steadfast. The central color in the midst of this castle wall is enduring hope to attain the grace that saves mankind. The red color above, burning to the sight, is the burning love of God and man, that gives great light. No wonder if this castle is wholly white within, for the heart of that maiden was never defiled with sin. The four towers, great and strong, so fair to see, were ghostly strength and soberness, righteousness and skill.[44] These four virtues drive out all manner of wickedness, and keep fast, within, all goodness.

The courts, one within another, in three stages, are clean maidenhood, motherhood, and true wifehood. There never was a woman except Saint Mary with all these three, but whosoever would be saved from sin, must have one of these. The seven barbicans we call the seven fair virtues, that suffered no vice to be in our Lady. Great meekness in her heart forever vanquished pride; envy could not abide her great charity; her devout abstinence destroyed all gluttony, and her clean maidenhood forbade lechery; wicked covetousness might never dwell in her heart, because wilful poverty guarded that castle; patience was always watching, so that the sin of wrath could never have resting place. There was in her heart so much spiritual comfort that the sin of sloth could never dwell therein. The fair well of the castle, that ever fills the ditches, is grace in God's mother, ever dear to sinful man. Thou who hast need of grace, go to the well-spring; whosoever has her help will never go to hell. Make the ditches of meekness and of good will, and the four streams of grace shall soon fill thee: one stream evermore shall wash thee clean of sin, another shall make thee steadfast against temptation, the third shall bear thee to bliss that is for aye. This well is evermore the spring of mercy and of pity. The throne of ivory is the soul of our sweet Lady; the seven steps leading thereto are the seven works of mercy; the rainbow of three colors bending over it is the might of the holy Trinity, covering her. No wonder if this castle is fair to see, since God, the sun of righteousness, would alight therein. He came through the closed gate just as the bright sunbeam comes and goes through the glass. All that man has need of is in this castle; he who has its help has happiness enough.

Translated by M. H. S.

BESTIARY

THE LION[45]

NATURE

I

The lion stands upon a hill, and if he hears a man hunting, or through his nostrils scents one approaching, he fills all his own footsteps, as he goes down to the dale, by drawing either dust or dew into them with his tail, so that the hunter cannot find him, and thus he speeds to his den and there shelters himself.

II

Another nature he has. When he is born he lies still and stirs not from sleep until the sun has shone thrice about him, then his father rouses him by the cry he makes.

III

The third habit the lion has is this: when he lies down to sleep he never closes the lids of his eyes.

SIGNIFICATION

I

Very high is that hill which is the kingdom of heaven; our Lord is the Lion, who lives there above. Though He chose to alight here on earth, the devil, even if he be a crafty hunter, could never know how He came down nor how He dwelt in that humble maiden, Mary by name, who bore Him for the salvation of men.

II, III

Though our Lord was dead, and buried, as was His will, and lay still in a stone until the third day, His father aided Him, so that He arose from the dead, to keep us alive. He watches, according to His will, as a shepherd, and we are the sheep; He will shield us if we hear His word, and go nowhere astray.

THE EAGLE

NATURE

I will make known to you the nature of the eagle, as I read about it in a book; how he renews his youth and how he emerges from old age when his limbs are unwieldy and his beak all twisted, and his flight is weak and his eyes dim; hear how he recreates himself. He seeks a well which springs up ever, both by night and by day; over that he flies, and up he soars until he passes through the sixth and the seventh skies and reaches heaven, and hovers as close as he can to the sun. The sun scorches his wings and makes his eyes bright; his feathers fall out because of the heat, and he falls down then into the water to the bottom of the well, where he becomes whole and sound and comes out all new, except that his beak is crooked. Since his beak is twisted, though his limbs are strong, he cannot procure food for himself. Then he goes to a stone and strikes his beak on it and continues to strike it until his beak loses all its crookedness, and at once with his straight bill he seizes what food he likes.

SIGNIFICATION

Man is like unto the eagle,—if you will listen,—old in his secret sins, ere he becomes a Christian. Before he had considered his sins his eyes were murky. Thus he may renew himself if he goes to church, and, there renouncing Satan and every sinful deed, betakes himself to Jesus Christ, who will be his reward. He believes in our Lord Christ, and learns the teachings of the priest, and the mist departs from his eyes while he lingers there. His hope is all fixed upon God, and he learns of His love which, like the sun, again restores his sight. Naked he falls in the font, and comes out all new, except for one little thing. What is that? His mouth is still untrue, his mouth is still unfamiliar with pater noster and creed. If he goes north or if he goes south he will soon discover his need; he will beg a favor from God and thus will make his mouth perfect; so may he gain his soul's food, through the grace of our Lord.

THE WHALE

NATURE

The whale is the largest fish that is in the ocean. You would say, if you should see it afloat, that it is an island, that sits upon the sea sand. When this fish, so unwieldy, is hungry he opens his jaws wide, and out of his throat comes a sweet odor, the sweetest thing that is on earth. When other fish perceive it they are glad to draw near; they come and hover in his mouth, unaware of his deceit. Then the whale shuts his jaws, sucking in all these fish. It is only the small ones he thus deceives; the big ones he cannot catch. This fish dwells at the bottom of the ocean, and lives there, always hale and well, until it comes to be the time when storms stir all the sea. Then summer and winter contend, and the whale cannot stay there, because the sea bottom is so turbid, so he rises and lies still, while the weather is so bad. Sailors in the ships driven about on the sea, dreading to die and anxious to live, look around and see this fish, and, believing it is an island, are very happy as they draw near; with all their strength they cast anchor, and go upon the island. By flint and steel they start a fire burning well on this wonder, and warm themselves, and eat and drink. The whale, feeling the fire, sinks them, for he quickly dives down to the bottom of the sea and thus drowns them all.

SIGNIFICATION

This devil is strong in wile and might, as witches are in their craft; he makes men hunger and thirst and have sinful desires; he entices men to him with his breath; whoever follows him finds shame. It is the ones of little faith whom he deceives, not those who are strong and steadfast in flesh and spirit, holding to the true faith. He who listens to the devil's teachings will at last repent it sorely; he who fastens his hope on him will follow him to dim hell.

THE SIREN

NATURE

In the sea are many wonders. The mermaid is like a maiden to the waist, but otherwise she is exactly like a fish with fins. This marvel dwells in dangerous places where the water is shallow, and she sinks ships and works harm thus. Merrily this maid sings, and she has many voices,—many and shrill,—but they are all evil, for sailors forget their steering because of her singing, and they slumber and sleep and wake too late; and the ships sink with the confusion, and come up nevermore. Wise men and wary know how to flee, and often escape with uncorrupted heart. By this maiden of whom you have heard, this monster half human and half fish, something is betokened.

SIGNIFICATION

Many men illustrate the meaning of this example: without, they wear the skin of sheep; within, they are wolves wholly; they speak piously, but wicked are their deeds; their deeds are all unlike what their mouths speak. Twofold they are in spirit,—they swear by the cross, by the sun, and by the moon, and they lie both in their speech and in their singing. They deceive thee then; they destroy thy goods with treachery and thy soul with lying.

Translated by M. H. S.

LAPIDARY

EXTRACTS FROM LAPIDARIES[46]

Evax, king of Arabia, sent to Nero, the emperor of Rome, a book which he had written concerning the nature of stones, telling their kinds, their names, their colors, in what lands they are found, and the virtues that they have. Many of their virtues are hidden, but others are well known. Doctors who know the powers of gems find them of great aid in their medicines. No wise man can doubt that God has placed great virtue in stones, as He has in herbs.

DIAMOND

The diamond is as clear as crystal, but it has also the aspect of steel. It is found in India. Such great hardness it has that neither with iron nor with fire can it be cut, but if it is soaked in the hot blood of a goat, a man can work it on the anvil with a hammer. The sharp splinters which are broken off are used to cut other gems. This stone is no bigger than a hazel-nut. In Arabia there is a kind of diamond, not so hard, which can be cut without goat's blood. It is not so beautiful nor so valuable as the other, although it is larger. A third species comes from Cypress, and a fourth from Greece. Each one has the power of attracting iron. Enchanters use this stone in their enchantments. It gives to the man who carries it strength and virtue; it protects him from bad dreams, from phantoms, from all poisons, and from all hates and discord; it cures madmen, and defends a man against his enemies. It should be set in gold or in silver, and worn upon the left arm.

SAPPHIRE

Sapphire is fit for the fingers of kings; it is resplendent and like the sky when free from clouds; there is no other stone which has greater virtue or beauty. Men call it Syrtites because it is found in the sand of Libya near the Syrtes. The best is that which is found in Turkey, for this is not translucent. It is of such great virtue that it is by right called the gem of all gems. It comforts the body and keeps its members whole; it overcomes envy and treachery, and it drives away fear. It frees a man from prison and looses heavy fetters; it is good for effecting reconciliation, and is better than any other stone for seeing in the water the signs which reveal things hitherto not known. As medicine it is valuable because it cools an internal fever; if a person dissolves it in milk it will cure bad diseases. It is good for the eyes, and for headache, and for disease of the tongue. He who carries it must be chaste.

Amethyst

The amethyst has a purple color, or sometimes is like violet or like drops of wine or like a rose. Some there are which turn almost white, others are like red wine mixed with water. From India it comes; it is easy to work, and it prevents intoxication. It would be precious if it were not so abundant, but it is commonplace since there is so much of it. There are five kinds.

Geratite

Geratite is black. It is of such a nature that if a man opens his mouth and puts the stone under his tongue he will divine what another person thinks of him, and can win any woman's devotion. This stone can be tried as follows: let a man anoint himself with milk and honey, go out into the sunshine where insects swarm, and if he has the stone in his mouth the insects will not attack him; if he removes the stone they will at once sting him.

Chelidonius

Chelidonius is a stone which one finds in the stomach of a swallow. It is not very beautiful, but it surpasses all the beautiful stones in usefulness. It is of ten sorts and of two colors—black and red. The red is good for the frenzy which seizes people who are moon-struck; it restores their sanity to madmen and cures those who are pining away. He who carries this stone will be a good orator and will be much beloved. One must carry it wrapped in linen cloth and suspended under the left arm. The black, if worn in the same way, aids a man to accomplish important things he has undertaken; it is also a help against the threats and rages of kings and princes. The water in which it is washed is helpful to diseased eyes. If wrapped in linen cloth of saffron tint, it drives away fever and restrains the humors which injure the body.

Coral

Coral is a stone which grows in the sea like a tree. It is green there where it grows, but when it is exposed to the air it hardens and becomes red. It is like a bush hardly half a foot high. It is very good to carry about, as say the authors Zoroaster and Metrodorus, for it protects one from lightning and tempest, and if one scatters it on vines or among olive trees, or upon a seeded field, it will be a protection from hail and other storms. It makes fruits multiply, it drives away phantoms, it gives a good beginning and a prosperous conclusion.

HELIOTROPE

Heliotrope is of such a nature that if one puts it in a basin of water opposite the sun, it makes the sun become red and creates an eclipse. In a little while it makes the water boil up over the basin's edge, and fall like a shower of rain. He who wears this can prophesy many things. It gives a man praise and good health, it stanches the flow of blood, it overcomes poison and treachery. Any one who takes the herb called heliotrope and binds the two together with the proper incantation can walk where he pleases and no one will see him. This stone comes from Ethiopia, from Cypress, and from Africa. It is very much like the emerald, but has red spots.

PEARL

The pearl is found in a shell, and it is called *unio* (union), because it is always found alone. The wise say that the oyster shells are open at certain times, and they receive the dew of heaven; the morning dews become white and clear pearls, while the evening dews are obscure. The young shells produce clearer pearls than the old ones do. The more dew the shells receive, the larger is the pearl, but no one is ever more than half an ounce in weight. If there is thunder when the dew is received, then the pearls perish. They grow in India and in Great Britain.

PANTHEROS

Pantheros is of various colors,—black, red, green, gray, purple, and rose color. All these shades appear in combination. Whoever sees it in the morning will not be defeated in battle, that day, nor in any other undertaking. In India there is a beast, of divers colors, called the panther, of whom other beasts are afraid, and this stone is named after him.

SYMBOLISM OF THE CARBUNCLE[47]

The carbuncle is red, and surpasses the wonders of all other stones. The books tell us that the gentle carbuncle, fine and clear, is the lord of all stones, the gem of all gems, and has the virtue of precious stones, above all. It is of such superiority, that when he who wears it comes among people, all accord him honor and grace, and rejoice in his coming. The books tell us that the beasts who drink of the stream where carbuncles have been washed, are cured of their malady; and the wretched who in good faith look at this stone are comforted and forget their adversity. By the virtue which God has sent, it soothes the eyes, comforts the heart and the body, and gives man lordship more than do those stones which are larger. Carbuncles are found in Libya in the river of paradise. The book of Moses says that God commanded that the carbuncle should be first in the second row of twelve stones. By night and by day it illumines all, and restores and lightens the heart. Sunlight does not take away any of its great and joy-giving color. Moses tells us that it signifies Jesus Christ, who came into the world to lighten our darkness, and Saint John, speaking of the coming of Jesus Christ, said He is the true Light who gives light to all men and to all the world. Isaiah the prophet said of Him that the people who walked in darkness have seen a great Light. Saint John did not find the carbuncle among the foundations of the celestial kingdom of Jerusalem, for all who desire to behold the carbuncle and the clearness of the true sun must turn to the true light of Jesus Christ.

SYMBOLISM OF THE TWELVE STONES[48]

Twelve stones there are in this world which have great significance. I shall not fail briefly to say what each one signifies. Red jasper signifies love; the green, faith; the white, sweetness. Sapphire means that he who has faith shall reign together with God. Chalcedony, which is the color of fire, shows who will be neighbors with God. Emerald signifies the faith which the Christians have in Him; sardonyx, chastity and humility among the saints; sardius, the sorrows which they had on earth for their love of God; chrysolite, the life celestial that they have after the life terrestrial; beryl, purification, which the saints pronounce to the people. Topaz signifies to us the crown of holy life; chrysoprase, the reward which holy men will hold very dear; and jacinth is a sign of the light which the saints have from the Creator. Amethyst shows the martyrdom which God suffered.

Translated by M. H. S.

HOMILY

CONCERNING MIRACLE PLAYS, GAMES, AND MINSTRELSY[49]

It is forbidden a clerk in orders to perform or to see miracle plays, for they are sinful gatherings and sights. He may, in church, play the resurrection, showing how God rose, and thus make men believe faithfully that Christ rose in flesh and blood, and he may play without harm the part showing how God was born in Yule night, and thus teach men to believe steadfastly that Christ was born of the Virgin Mary. If he plays parts in the streets or in groves, it seems truly a sinful sight. Saint Isidore bears witness to this, for he says, "These men forsake what they accepted,—God and Christianity, when they take part in such things as miracle plays or in games or tournaments of great price." These are pomps that thou didst forsake when thou didst accept Christianity. At the font the ignorant man says, "I forsake thee, here, Satan, and all thy pomps and thy works." This is the instruction thou hast had as a clerk. Hast thou kept thy promise when thou dost take part in such performances? Thou hast broken thy covenant with God, and dost serve thy sire, Termagant. Saint Isidore says in his writings, "All those who delight in seeing such things, or who lend horse or harness for them, are perilously guilty." If a priest or a clerk lends a vestment which has been hallowed by the sacrament, he, more than others, is to be blamed, for he shall have the infamy which attends sacrilege, and shall be chastised as is right.

Dances, carols, and summer games bring shame in many ways; when thou dost plan to take part in these thou art slothful in God's service, and shalt be punished for thy sin.

What say you of minstrels, all of whom delight in such things? Their deeds are full of peril, and dear neither to God nor to God's house. They would rather hear of a dance or of deeds of boasting and of pride than any good of God in heaven, or other wisdom that may be named. In folly is spent all that they get,—on their dress, their drink, and their meat. And because of such things, I shall tell you what once befell a minstrel. Saint Gregory tells this story:

A minstrel, a goliardys,[50] came once to a bishop's house, and asked for charity. The porter let him enter. At meal time the board was laid; and when the benison should have been said, this minstrel made melody with music loud and high. By report, the bishop was a holy man. He sat down at the table, and should have blessed the food, with a word, but he was so disturbed by the noise of the minstrelsy that he did not say grace, as he usually did, very devoutly.

The bishop complained sorely, and said to all those who were there that he would not put the benison above the grace of charity. He saw well, in spirit, that vengeance was approaching speedily, and said, "Give him his alms, and let him go. Death approaches, which will slay him." The minstrel received charity, and then departed, and as he passed out of the gate, a stone fell down from the wall, and slew him there. That betokened that God was not pleased with what the minstrel did, when he disturbed the devotion of the good man.

This is told for the sake of gleemen, so that they will take some heed as to where it is proper to make music, and also for the sake of those who listen, so that they will not love minstrelsy too dearly, nor have for it such affection that they will worship heaven's King the less.

I shall tell you what I have heard of this bishop, Saint Robert, whose surname is Grossteste of Lincoln. He loved to hear the harp, for it makes the wit of man keen. Next his chamber, beside his study, was his harper's chamber. Many times, by night and by day, he found solace in notes and lays. Some one asked him why he had such delight in minstrelsy, and he told why he held the harper dear: "The virtue of the harp will destroy the fiend's might, and rightly the harp is likened to the cross. Another thing comforts me,—if God has given to a piece of wood the power to make men hear so much joy, even more joy, there must be where God Himself dwells. The harp often reminds me of the joy and bliss where God is. Therefore, good men, you should learn when you hear a gleeman, to worship God with all your might, according as David says in the Psalter, 'in harp, in tabor, and in symphony, worship God; in trumpets and psaltery, in stringed instruments and organs, and in bells ringing, in all these worship heaven's King.' If you do thus, I say boldly, you may hear your minstrelsy."

Translated by M. H. S.

SATIRE

THE SONG OF THE UNIVERSITY OF PARIS[51]

Much argument is heard of late,
The subject I'll attempt to state,
A question for dispute, I fear,
That will hang on for many a year.
The student-folk of Paris town
(I speak of those in cap and gown,
Students of art, philosophy,—
In short, "the University,"
And not our old-time learned men)
Have stirred up trouble here again.
Nothing they'll gain, it seems to me,
Except more bitter enmity,
Till there is no peace, day or night.
Does such a state of things seem right?

To give his son a chance to stay
In Paris, growing wise each day,
Is some old peasant's one ambition.
To pay his bills and his tuition
The poor hard-working father slaves;
Sends him each farthing that he saves,
While he in misery will stay
On his scant plot of land to pray

That his hard toil may help to raise
His son to honor and to praise.

But once the son is safe in town
 The story then reads upside down.
Forgetting all his pledges now,
The earnings of his father's plow
He spends for weapons, not for books.
Dawdling through city streets, he looks
To find some pretty, loitering wench,
Or idle brawl by tavern bench;
Wanders at will and pries about,
Till money fails and gown wears out.—
Then he starts fresh on the old round;
Why sow good seed on barren ground?
Even in Lent when men should do
Something pleasing in God's view,
Your students then elect to wear
For penitence, no shirts of hair,
But swaggering hauberks, as they sit
Drowning in drink their feeble wit;
While three or four of them excite
Four hundred students to a fight,
And close the University.
(Not such a great calamity!)

Yet, heavens, for one of serious mind
What life more pleasing can you find
Than earnest scholar's life may be?
More pains than precious gems has he,
And while he's struggling to grow wise,

Amusements he must sacrifice,—
Give up his feasting and his drinking,
And spend his time in sober thinking.
His life is just about as merry
 As is a monk's in a monastery.
Why send a boy away to school
There to become an arrant fool?
When he should be acquiring sense,
He wastes his time and all his pence,
And to his friends brings only shame,
While they suppose him winning fame.

Translated by Marion E. Markley

THE LAND OF COCKAYGNE[52]

Far in the sea west of Spain is a land called Cockaygne. There is no land except the kingdom of heaven its equal in happiness and goodness; though paradise is joyful and bright, Cockaygne is still fairer. What is there in paradise but grass and flowers and green branches? Though joy and great pleasure are in paradise, yet there is no food but fruit; there is no hall, no bower, no bench, and nothing but water to quench one's thirst. Only two men live there, Enoch and Elias; a wretched life must they lead where no other men dwell.

In Cockayne is meat and drink, without care or trouble or toil. The meat is dainty; the drink is pure wine at noon and at supper. This land has no peer on earth; verily there is no place under heaven so full of joy and bliss.

In that land is many a sweet sight; it is always day and never night; there is no strife nor quarrel; there is no death, but only lasting life; there is no lack of food nor dress; there is no angry man nor woman; there is no serpent, wolf, nor fox, horse nor colt, ox nor cow; there is no sheep nor swine nor goat nor steed nor stables. There are no flies nor fleas nor other insects in town or bed or house, no serpents nor snails, nor is there thunder, sleet, nor hail, storm, rain, nor wind; there is no blind man nor woman, but everywhere is jest and joy and glee. Well fares it with him who there may dwell.

Rivers flow there, wide and fair, of oil, of milk, of honey, and of wine. Water serves there only two uses,—to look at, and to use for washing. There are many kinds of fruit, and everywhere is solace and delight.

There is a fair abbey of white monks and of gray; there are bowers and halls; the walls are all of pasties, of flesh, of fish, and of rich meats,—the very best a man may eat. Flour cakes are the shingles of church, cloister, bower, and hall. The pinnacles are fat puddings, rich food for princes and kings; men may eat as much as they please, without any danger. All things are in common to both old and young, to strong and weak, to meek and bold.

There is a cloister fair and light, broad and long and beautiful. All the pillars of that cloister are of crystal, with bases and capitals of green jasper and red coral. In the meadow is a tree, most pleasing to the sight. The root is ginger and galingale; the shoots are all of zedoary; the finest maces are the flowers; the rind is sweet smelling cinnamon; and the fruit is clove of goodly taste. Cubebs are not lacking, either. There are roses red of hue, and lilies, also, fair to see. They never fade by day nor by night, this should be a pleasant sight. There are four wells in the abbey, made of triacle and aromatic plants, of balm and also of spiced wine, ever fed by underground streams. Precious stones and gold are there, sapphire, pearl, carbuncle, astrion, emerald, liguros and chrysoprase, beryl, onyx and topaz, amethyst and chrysolite, chalcedony and epetite. There are many birds,—the throstle, thrush, and nightingale, the lark and the woodpecker, and other birds without number, that never cease singing merrily day nor night.

More, however, there is to tell you; geese roasted on the spit fly to that abbey and cry: "Geese, all hot, all hot." They bring plenty of garlick, the best you could ever look for. The larks, that are familiar food, light in a man's mouth, all stewed daintily and powdered with clove and cinnamon. There is never any question of drink, but every one takes enough, yet does not toil.

When the monks go to mass, all the glass windows turn to bright crystal, to give the monks more light. When the masses are all said, the crystal turns again to glass, in the state that it was before.... [The rest of the poem satirizes the morals of the monks.]

Translated by M. H. S.

THE COMPLAINT OF THE HUSBANDMAN[53]

I heard men upon earth make many a moan,

Of how they were harried in their task of tilling:

Good years and grain are both of them gone,

We enjoy here no tales, and have no song to sing.

Now we must work, no way else is known,

I may no longer live by my gleaning.

Yet even a bitterer demand has upgrown,

For ever the fourth penny goes to the king.

Thus we complain of the king and have cares that are cold;

Though we dream of recovery we are ever downcast.

He who has any goods which he hoped he could hold

Learns that what we love most we must lose at the last.

Loath are we to lose what little there is,

And we have our henchmen who will for pay sue.

The hayward[54] bodes harm if we have aught of his,

The bailiff[55] with blows shows how well he can do,

The woodward[56] awaits in the watched wilderness:

Neither riches nor rest will arise for us few.

Thus they pillage the poor, who have little of bliss,

And must sweat at their toil and waste away too.

He must needs waste away, whatever he swore,

Who hath not a hood his own head to hide.

Thus will walks in the land, and law is no more,

And picked from the poor is the persecutor's pride.

Thus they pillage the poor and pick them all clean,

 And the rich men are ruling without any right;

Their lands and their people all lie very lean,

Through demands of the bailiffs such sorrows alight.
Men of religion[57] are abject and mean
As are baron and bondman,[58] the clerk and the knight.
Thus will walks in the land and sorrow is seen,
Falsehood grows fat and mars all with his might.

He stands still in a spot and shows a stern soul,
Who makes beggars wander with long staves and bags;
Thus we are hunted from hall and from hole,
And those who wore robes are now wearing rags.

And then come the beadles[59] with many a boast:
"Supply me with silver for the green wax,[60]
Thou art set down in my writ as thou thyself know'st,"
Yet more than ten times have I paid my tax.
Then I must furnish hens for the roast,
And fairly, each fish day, have lamprey and lax.[61]
If I go to the market, I lose, at the most,
Though I sell my bill[62] and my big axe.

I may place my pledge well if I will,
Or sell my corn when it's green as the grass;
Yet I am a foul churl, though they have their fill;
What I've saved all the year I must spend at this pass.

Needs must I spend what I've saved from of yore,
Against the coming of catchpoles I must take care;

The master beadle comes in like a brutish boar
 And says he will make my dwelling all bare,
So then I must bribe him, with one mark or more,
Although I at the set day should sell my own mare;
Thus the green wax grieves us neath our garments poor,

So that men hunt us as hound does the hare.

They hunt us as hound does a hare on a hill;
Since I took to the land such woe I've been taught.
The beadles have never had quite all their fill,
For they slip away, and it's we who are caught.

Thus I catch and I carry cares that are cold,
Since I have had cottage and reckoning to keep.
To seek silver for the king, my seed I have sold,
And my land has lain fallow and learned how to sleep.
Since they took my fair cattle away from the fold,
When I think of old joys I am ready to weep;
Thus are bred so many of these beggars bold,
And our rye is rotten and rank ere we reap.

Rank is our rye and rotten in the straw,
Because of foul weather by brook and by shore;
Thus wakes in this world the worst woe men e'er saw,
As well waste all away, as work thus evermore.

Translated by M. H. S.

SIR PENNY[63]

On earth there is a little thing
That reigns as does the richest king,
In this and every land;
Sir Penny is his name, we're told,
He compels both young and old
To bow unto his hand.

Popes and kings and emperors,
Bishops, abbots, too, and priors,
Parson, priest, and knight,
Barons, earls, and dukes, also,
Gladly in his service go,
Both by day and night.

Sir Penny changes a man's mood
And makes him, often, don his hood
And rise and stand again.
Men honor him with reverence
And give utmost obedience
Unto that little swain.

In the king's court it is no gain
Against Sir Penny to complain,
So great is he in might;
He is so witty and so strong
That be a matter ever so wrong
He will make it right.

With Penny women may be won
 By those men they once did shun,
As often may be seen;
Long with him they will not chide,
For he can help them trail aside,
In good scarlet and green.

He may buy both heaven and hell
And everything there is to sell,
Such grace he has on earth.
He may loose and he may bind;

The poor are ever put behind,
When he comes to a place.

When he begins to take control,
He makes meek the cruel soul
And weak who bold has been;
All men's needs are quickly sped,
Without pledge or bail to dread,
Where he is go-between.

The justices he makes so blind
They are unable right to find
Or even truth to see;
To give judgment they are loath,
If it should make Sir Penny wroth,
For dear to them is he.

Where strife was, Penny soon makes peace;
From anger he will bring release,
As long as men will spend;
Of foes he makes friends most true,
 His counsel they will never rue
Who have him for friend.

That lord is set above us all
And richly served within the hall
At the festal board;
The more he gives men plenteously,
The more beloved always is he,
And, by a host, adored.

He makes many be forsworn
Who in body and soul are made forlorn

By following after him.
Other god they will not have,
Except that little and round knave,
To end their sorrows grim.

On him alone they set their hearts,
And no man from his love departs,
Neither for good nor ill.
All that he will on earth have done
Is granted soon by everyone
According to his will.

Penny is a good fellow;
Men greet him in deed and word, also,
Whenever he comes near;
He is not welcomed as a guest,
But always served with what is best,
A soft seat and good cheer.

Whoever falls in any need,
With Penny's help will win good speed,
Whatever may betide;
He that is Penny's friend, withal,
Shall have his will in steed and stall
When others are set aside.

Sir Penny gives men richest weeds,
And many men may ride his steeds
In this world so wide.
In every game and every play
The mastery is given aye
To Penny for his pride.

Sir Penny always wins the prize
Wherever towers and castles rise
By town or country way;
Without either spear or shield
He is the best in wood or field,
Most stalwart in the fray.

In every place this truth is seen,
Sir Penny rules both great and mean;
Most masterful is he;
And all is as he does command;
Against his will no man dare stand,
Neither on land or sea.

Sir Penny's counsel gives great aid
To those who have his law obeyed,
As the assizes show.
He lengthens life and saves from death,
 But love him not o'er well, God saith,
For covetousness is woe.

If thou shouldst chance treasure to win,
Delight thee not too much therein,
Nor proud nor haughty be;
But spend all as a Christian can,
So that thou mayst love God and man
In perfect charity.

God grant us grace, with heart and will,
The goods that he is giving, still
Well and wisely to spend;
And our lives here so to lead,

That we may have His bliss for meed,
Ever without an end.

Translated by M. H. S.

LAY

SIR ORFEO[64]

Orfeo was a king,
In Inglond an heighe lording,
A stalworth man and hardi bo,[65]
Large and curteys, he was al so;
His fader was comen of king Pluto,
And his moder of king Juno,
That sum time were as godes y hold,
For aventours that thai dede and told.
This king sojurned in Traciens,
That was a cite of noble defens,
For Winchester was cleped[66] tho
Traciens, with outen no.
The king hadde a quen of priis,
That was y cleped dame Heurodis.
The fairest levedi[67] for the nones[68]
That might gon on bodi and bones,
Ful of love and godenisse
Ac no man may telle hir fairnise.
Bifel so in the comessing of May,
When miri and hot is the day,
And oway beth winter schours,
And everi feld is ful of flours,
And blosme breme[69] on everi bough,

Over al wexeth miri anough,

This ich[70] quen dame Heurodis,

Tok to maidens of priis,

 And went in an undren tide[71]

To play bi an orchard side

To se the floures sprede and spring,

And to here the foules sing:

Thai sett hem doun al thre,

Under a fair ympe[72] tre,

And wel sone this fair quene,

Fel on slepe opon the grene.

The maidens durst hir nought awake,

Bot let hir ligge and rest take,

So sche slepe til after none,

That under tide was al y done;

Ac as sone as sche gan awake,

Sche crid and lothli bere gan make;

Sche froted[73] hir honden and hir fet,

And crached her visage, it blede wete,

Hir riche robe hye al to rett,[74]

And was reneyd[75] out of hir witt.

The two maidens hir biside

No durst with hir no leng abide,

But ourn[76] to the palays ful right,

And told bothe squier and knight,

That her quen awede[77] wold,

And bad hem go and hir at hold.

Knightes urn[76], and levedis al so,

Damisels sexti and mo,

In the orchard to the quen hye come,
And her up in her armes nome,[78]
And brought hir to bed attelast,
 And held hir there fine fast;
Ac ever sche held in o cri
And wold up and owy.
When Orfeo herd that tiding
Never him nas wers for no thing;
He come with knightes tene
To chaumber right bifor the quene,
And biheld and seyd with grete pite:
O lef[79] liif, what is te,[80]
That ever yete hast ben so stille,
And now gredest[81] wonder schille[82];
Thi bodi, that was so white y core,[83]
With thine nailes is al to tore,
Allas! thi rode,[84] that was so red,
Is al wan as thou were ded;
And also thine fingres smale,
Beth al blodi and al pale;
Allas! thi lovesum eyghen[85] to
Loketh so man doth on his fo;
A dame, Ich biseche merci,
Let ben al this reweful cri,
And tel me what the is, and hou,
And what thing may the help now?
Tho lay sche stille attelast,
And gan to wepe swithe[86] fast,
And seyd thus the king to:

Allas! mi lord, sir Orfeo,
Seththen[87] we first to gider were,
Ones wroth never we nere,
 Bot ever Ich have y loved the
As mi liif, and so thou me,
Ac now we mot[88] delen ato,
Do thi best, for y mot go.
Allas! quath he, forlorn Ich am,
Whider wiltow go and to wham?
Whider thou gost Ichil with the,
And whider Y go thou schalt with me.
Nay, nay, sir, that nought nis,
Ichil the telle al how it is:
As Ich lay this under tide,
And slepe under our orchard side,
Ther come to me to fair knightes
Wele y armed al to rightes,
And bad me comen an heighing,[89]
And speke with her lord the king;
And Ich answerd at wordes bold,
Y durst nought, no y nold.
Thai priked oghain[90] as thai might drive,
Tho com her king also blive,
With an hundred knightes and mo,
And damissels an hundred al so;
Al on snowe white stedes,
As white as milke were her wedes,
Y no seighe never yete bifore
So fair creatours y core!

The king hadde a croun on hed,
It nas of silver, no of gold red,
Ac it was of a precious ston;
As bright as the sonne it schon:
 And as son as he to me cam,
Wold Ich, nold Ich, he me nam,
And made me with him ride,
Opon a palfray bi his side,
And brought me to his pallays,
Wele atird in ich ways;
And schewed me castels and tours,
Rivers, forestes, frith[91] with flours;
And his riche stedes[92] ichon,
And seththen me brought oghain hom,
In to our owhen orchard,
And said to me after ward:
Loke dame, to morwe thatow be
Right here under this ympe tre;
And than thou schalt with ous go
And live with ous ever mo,
And yif thou makest ous y let,
Where thou be, thou worst y fet[93]
And to tore thine limes al,
That nothing help the no schal,
And thei thou best so to torn
Yete thou worst with ous y born.
When king Orfeo herd this cas,
O we![94] quath he, allas! allas!
Lever me were to lete[95] mi liif,

Than thus to lese the quen mi wiif,
He asked conseyl at ich man,
Ac no man him help no can.
A morwe the under tide is come
And Orfeo hath his armes y nome,
 And wele ten hundred knightes with him,
Ich y armed stout and grim;
And with the quen wenten he,
Right unto that ympe tre.
Thai made scheltrom[96] in ich aside,
And sayd thai wold ther abide,
And dye ther everichon,
Er the quen schuld fram hem gon:
Ac yete amiddes hem ful right,
The quen was oway y twight,[97]
With fairi forth y nome,
Men wist never wher sche was bicome.
Tho was ther criing, wepe and wo,
The king into his chamber is go,
And oft swoned opon the ston
And made swiche diol[98] and swiche mon,
That neighe his liif was y spent;
Ther was non amendement.
He cleped to gider his barouns,
Erls, lordes of renouns,
And when thai al y comen were:
Lordinges, he said, bifor you here
Ich ordainy min heigh steward
To wite[99] mi kingdom after ward,

In mi stede ben he schal,
To kepe mi londes over al,
For now Ichave mi quen y lore,[100]
The fairest levedi that ever was bore;
Never eft y nil no woman se,
Into wildernes Ichil te,[101]
 And live ther ever more,
With wilde bestes in holtes[102] hore;
And when ye under stond that y be spent,
Make you than a parlement,
And chese you a newe king:
Now doth your best with al mi thing.
Tho was ther wepeing in the halle,
And grete cri among hem alle;
Unnethe[103] might old or yong
For wepeing speke a word with tong.
Thai kneled adoun al y fere,[104]
And praid him yif his wille were,
That he no schuld nought from hem go.
Do way! quath he, it schal be so:
All his kingdom he forsoke,
But a sclavin[105] on him he toke;
He no hadde kirtel, no hode,
Schert, no nother gode,
Bot his harp he toke algate,[106]
And dede him barfot out atte gate:
No man most with him go.
O way! what ther was wepe and wo,
When he that hadde ben king with croun,

Went so poverlich out of toun.
Thurch wode, and over heth,
Into the wildernes he geth,
Nothing he fint that him is ays,[107]
Bot ever he liveth in gret malais[108];
He that hadde y werd the fowel[109] and griis,[110]
 And on bed the purper biis,[111]
Now on hard hethe he lith,
With leves and gresse he him writh[112]:
He that hadde castels, and tours,
River, forest, frith with flours;
Now, thei it commenci to snewe and frese,
This king mot make his bed in mese[113]:
He that had y had knightes of priis.
Bifor him kneland, and levedis,
Now seth he no thing that him liketh,
Bot wild wormes by him striketh:
He that had y had plente
Of mete and drink, of ich deynte,
Now may he al day digge and wrote,[114]
Er he finde his fille of rote;
In somer he liveth bi wild frut,
And berren, bot gode lite;
In winter may he no thing finde,
Bot rote, grases, and the rinde;
Al his bodi was oway dwine
For missays, and al to chine,[115]
Lord! who may telle the sore
This king sufferd ten yere and more:

His here of his berd, blac and rowe,[116]
To his girdel stede was growe;
His harp, where on was al his gle,
He hidde in an holwe tre;
And, when the weder was clere and bright,
He toke his harp to him wel right,
And harped at his owhen wille,
Into alle the wode the soun gan schille,
That alle the wilde bestes that ther beth,
For joie abouten him thai teth[117];
And all the foules that ther were,
Come and sete on ich a brere;
To here his harping a fine,[118]
So miche melody was ther in.
And when he his harping lete wold,
No best bi him abide nold.
He might se besides
Oft in hot under tides,
The king o fairy, with his rout,
Com to hunt him al about:
With dim cri and bloweing,
And houndes also with him berking;
Ac no best thai no nome,
No never he nist whider thai bi come.
And other while he might him se
As a gret ost bi him te,
Wele atourned[119] ten hundred knightes,
Ich y armed to his rightes;
Of cuntenaunce stout and fers,

With mani displaid baners;
And ich his swerd y drawe hold:
Ac never he nist whider thai wold.
And other while he seighe other thing:
Knightes and levedis com daunceing,
In queynt atire gisely,
Queyitt pas, and softly:
Tabours and trimpes yede him bi,
And al maner menstraci.
And on a day he seighe him biside
Sexti levdis on hors ride,
Gentil and jolif, as brid on ris[120];
Nought o man amonges hem ther nis;
And ich a faucoun on hond bere,
And riden on haukin bi o rivere,
Of game thai founde wel gode haunt,
Maulardes, hayroun, and cormeraunt;
The foules of the water ariseth,
The faucouns hem wele deviseth,
Ich faucoun his pray slough:
That seighe Orfeo, and lough.
Par fay, quath he, ther is fair game!
Thider Ichil bi Godes name,
Ich was y won[121] swiche werk to se.
He aros, and thider gan te;
To a levedi he was y come,
Biheld, and hath wele under nome,
And seth, bi al thing, that it is
His owhen quen dam Heurodis.

Yern he biheld hir, and sche him eke,
Ac noither to other a word no speke:
For messais that sche on him seighe,
That had ben so riche and so heighe,
The teres fel out of her eighe;
The other levedis this y seighe,
And maked hir oway to ride,
Sche most with him no lenger abide.
 Allas! quath he, now me is wo!
Whi nil deth now me slo,
Allas! wroche, that Y no might
Dye now, after this sight!
Allas! to long last mi liif
When Y no dar nought with mi wiif,
No hye to me, o word speke,
Allas! whi nil min hert breke!
Parfay, quath he, tide what bitide,
Whider so this levedis ride,
The selve way Ichil streche,
Of liif, no deth, me no reche.
His sclavin he dede on, all so spac,[122]
And henge his harp upon his bac,
And had wel gode will to gon;
He no spard noither stub no ston.
In at a roche the levedis rideth,
And he after, and nought abideth;
When he was in the roche y go,
Wele thre mile, other mo,
He com in to a fair cuntray,

As bright so sonne on somers day,
Smothe, and plain, and al grene;
Hille, no dale nas ther non y sene;
Amidde the lond a castel he sighe,
Riche, and real,[123] and wonder heighe;
Al the ut mast wal,
Was cler and schine as cristal;
And hundred tours ther were about,
Degiselich[124] and bataild stout;
The butras com out of the diche,
Of rede gold y arched riche,
The bonsour[125] was avowed[126] al,
Of ich maner divers animal;
With in ther wer wide wones,[127]
Al of precious stones,
The werst piler on to biholde,
Was al of burnist gold;
Al that lond was ever light,
For when it schuld be therk[128] and night,
The riche stones[129] light gonne,
As bright as doth at none the sonne,
No man may telle, no thenche in thought,
The riche werk that ther was wrought,
Bi al thing, him think that it is
The proude court of paradis.
In this castel the levedis alight,
He wold in after, yif he might.
Orfeo knokketh atte gate,
The porter was redi ther ate,

And asked, what he wold have y do.
Parfay, quath he, Icham a minstrel lo,
To solas thi lord with my gle,
Yif his swete wille be.
The porter undede the gate anon,
And lete him in to the castel gon.
Than he gan bihold about al,
And seighe full liggeand[130] with in the wal,
Of folk that were thider y brought,
 And thought dede and nare nought:
Sum stode with outen hade[131];
And sum on armes nade;[132]
And sum thurch the bodi hadde wounde;
And sum lay wode[133] y bounde;
And sum armed on hors sete;
And sum astrangled as thai ete;
And sum were in water adreynt[134];
And sum with fire al for schreynt[135];
Wives ther lay on child bedde;
Sum ded, and sum awedde[136];
And wonder fele ther lay bisides,
Right as thai slepe her under tides;
Eche was thus in this warld y nome,
With fairi thider y come.
Ther he seighe his owhen wiif,
Dame Heurodis his liif liif
Slepe under an ympe tre;
Bi her clothes he knewe that it was he.
And when he hadde bihold this mervails alle,

He went in to the kinges halle;
Then seighe he ther a semly sight,
A tabernacle blisseful and bright
Ther in her maister king sete,
And her quen fair and swete;
Her crounes, her clothes, schine so bright,
That unnethe bihold he hem might.
When he hadde biholden al that thing,
He kneled adoun bifor the king;
O Lord, he seyd, yif it thi wille were,
 Mi menstraci thou schust y here.
The king answerd, what man artow,
That art hider y comen now?
Ich, no non that is with me,
No sent never after the.
Seththen that ich here regni gan,
Y no fond never so fole hardi man
That hider to ous durst wende,
Bot that Ichim walde of sende.
Lord, quath he, trowe ful wel,
Y nam bot a pover menstrel,
And, sir, it is the maner of us,
To seche mani a lordes hous,
Thei we nought welcom no be,
Yete we mot proferi forth our gle.
Bifor the king he sat adoun
And tok his harp so miri of soun,
And tempreth his harp as he wel can,
And blisseful notes he ther gan,

That al that in the paleys were,
Com to him for to here,
And liggeth adoun to his fete,
Hem thenketh his melody so swete.
The king herkneth, and sitt ful stille,
To here his gle he hath gode wille.
Gode bourde[137] he hadde of his gle,
The riche quen al so hadde he.
When he hadde stint[138] his harping,
Than seyd to him the king,
Menstrel, me liketh wele thi gle,
 Now aske of me what it be,
Largelich Ichil the pay,
Now speke, and tow might asay.
Sir, he seyd, Ich beseche the,
Thatow woldest give me,
That ich levedi bright on ble,[139]
That slepeth under the ympe tre.
Nay, quath the king, that nought nere,
A sori couple of you it were,
For thou art lene, rowe, and blac,
And sche is lovesome with outen lac;
A lothlich thing it were forthi,[140]
To sen hir in thi compayni.
O sir, he seyd, gentil king,
Yete were it a wele fouler thing
To here a lesing[141] of thy mouthe,
So, sir, as ye seyd nouthe,[142]
What Ich wold aski have Y schold;

And nedes thou most thi word hold.

The king seyd, seththen it is so,

Take hir bi the hand, and go;

Of hir Ichil thatow be blithe.

He kneled adoun, and thonked him swithe.[143]

His wiif he tok bi the hond

And dede him swithe[144] out of that lond;

And went him out of that thede,[145]

Right as he came the way he yede.[146]

So long he hath the way y nome,

To Winchester he is y come,

 That was his owhen cite,

Ac no man knewe that it was he,

No forther than the tounes ende,

For knoweleche no durst wende,

Bot with a begger y bilt ful narwe,

Ther he tok his herbarwe,[147]

To him, and to his owhen wiif,

As a minstrel of pover liif,

And asked tidings of that lond,

And who the kingdom held in hond.

The pover begger, in his cote,[148]

Told him everich a grot[149]

How her quen was stole owy,

Ten yer gon with fairy,

And how her king en exile yede,

Bot no man niste in wiche thede,

And how the steward the lond gan hold,

And other mani thinges him told.

A morwe ogain none tide
He maked his wiif ther abide,
The beggers clothes he borwed anon,
And heng his harp his rigg[150] opon,
And went him in to that cite,
That men might him bi hold and se.
Erls, and barouns bold,
Burjays, and levedis, him gun bi hold;
Lo! thai seyd, swiche a man,
Hou long the here hongeth him opan!
Lo! hou his berd hongeth to his kne,
He is y clongen[151] al so a tre.
 And as he yede in the strete,
With his steward he gan mete,
And loude he sett on him a crie,
Sir steward, he seyd, merci,
Icham an harpour of hethenisse,
Helpe me now in this distresse!
The steward seyd, com with me, come,
Of that Ichave thou schalt have some;
Everich gode harpour is welcom me to,
For mi lordes love, sir Orfeo.
In the castel the steward sat atte mete,
And mani lording was bi him sete;
There were trompour and tabourers,
Harpours fele, and crouders,[152]
Miche melody thai maked alle,
And Orfeo sat stille in the halle,
And herkneth when thai ben al stille,

He toke his harp and tempred schille,
The blifulest notes he herped there,
That ever ani man y herd with ere,
Ich man liked wel his gle.
The steward biheld and gan y se,
And knewe the harp als blive;
Menstrel, he seyd, so mot thou thrive,
Where hadestow this harp, and hou?
Ypray that thou me telle now.
Lord, quath he, in uncouthe thede,
Thurch a wildernes as Y yede;
Ther Y founde in a dale,
With lyouns a man to torn smale,
And wolves him frete[153] with teth so scharp;
Bi him Y found this ich harp,
Wele ten yere it is y go.
O! quath the steward, now me is wo!
That was mi lord, sir Orfeo!
Allas! wreche what schall Y do,
That have swiche a lord y lore,[154]
A way, that Ich was y bore,
That him was so hard grace y yarked,[155]
And so vile deth y marked!
Adoun he fel aswon to grounde,
His barouns him tok up in that stounde,[156]
And telleth him hou it geth,
It is no bot[157] of mannes deth.
King Orfeo knewe wel bi than,
His steward was a trewe man,

And loved him as he aught to do,
And stont up, and seyt thus lo,
Steward, herkne now this thing,
Yif Ich were Orfeo the king,
And hadde y suffred ful yore,
In wildernisse miche sore;
And hadde y won mi quen owy,
Out of the lond of fairy;
And hadde y brought the levedi hende,[158]
Right here to the tounes ende,
And with a begger her in[159] y nome,
And were mi self hider y come,
Poverlich to the thus stille,
For to asay thi gode wille;
 And Ich founde the thus trewe,
Thou no schust it never rewe,
Sikerlich for love, or ay,[160]
Thou schust be king after mi day,
And yif thou of my deth hadest ben blithe,
Thou schust have voided al so swithe.
Tho al tho that ther in sete,
That it was king Orfeo under gete,[161]
And the steward him wele knewe,
Over and over the bord[162] he threwe,
And fel adoun to his fet;
So dede everich lord that ther sete,
And al thai sayd at o criing,
Ye beth our lord, sir, and our king.
Glad thai were of his live,

To chaumber thai ladde him als bilive,[163]
And bathed him and schaved his berd,
And tired him as a king apert[164];
And seththen with gret processioun,
Thai brought the quen in to the toun,
With al maner menstraci;
Lord, ther was grete melody!
For joie thai wepe with her eighe;
That hem so sounde y comen seighe.
Now king Orfeo newe coround is,
And his quen dame Heurodis;
And lived long afterward;
And seththen was king the steward.
Harpours in Bretaine after than
Herd hou this mervaile bigan,
 And made her of a lay of gode likeing,
And nempned[165] it after the king.
That lay Orfeo is y hote[166];
Gode is the lay, swete is the note.
Thus com sir Orfeo out of his care;
God graunt ous alle wele to fare! Amen.

NOTES

Frontispiece.

"Last Judgment" is an early work by Fra Angelico (1387-1455), who was a member of the Dominican order, and who spent his monastic leisure in painting visionary scenes. The picture represents Christ on the judgment seat, encircled by cherubim and seraphim, with saints and apostles seated on either side. Below are open graves. On His left devils are driving sinners into hideous torments; on His right angels are conducting the blessed across the flowery meadows of the earthly paradise toward the gleaming gates of the celestial city. The detail given here is sometimes called "The Dance of the Angels." The robes of the angelic beings who go singing and caroling are in the colors characteristic of Fra Angelico,—azure, green, and rose, irradiated by countless golden stars.

PROEM

OF MAN'S BODY. OF MAN'S SOUL

This introductory bit of mediæval lore is translated from "Cursor Mundi" (Over-runner of the World), a long poem, probably written in the early fourteenth century. The author says plainly at the beginning of his work that he is vying with romances and other secular tales which draw the thoughts of men away from spiritual matters. The poem, written in 24,000 verses in the short couplet, tells the history of the seven ages of the world, from the Creation to Doomsday, covering very much the same matter as that presented in the miracle plays. The "Cursor Mundi" has been edited by R. Morris for the Early English Text Society. Lines 511-584 are here translated.

DEBATE

THE AMOROUS CONTENTION OF PHILLIS AND FLORA

"De Phillide et Flora," a Latin poem of the twelfth century, perhaps, was translated about 1595 by George Chapman. In 1598 a certain "R. S." republished this translation with a few minor changes, but the work is essentially Chapman's. The present reprint follows the text in Thomas Wright's "Latin Poems commonly attributed to Walter Mapes." Camden Society, Vol. XVI. London, 1841. The translation reproduces the stanza and rime form of the original. Although the Elizabethan language may present some difficulties, they are not very serious to any one who will read slowly enough to enjoy "the proud full sail of his great verse" who may have been the rival of Shakespeare, and who was certainly one of the inspirers of John Keats.

The poem itself is of significance because, as forerunner of poems of the order of "The Romance of the Rose," it illustrates significant mediæval traits. The attitude towards nature, classicism, love, war, and learning is of great interest, and so, too, is the position of women in that sophisticated world. The disputation gives a pretty picture of the seriousness of feminine thought. The account of the court of the god of love and the power ascribed to him are a good introduction to the conventions of love poetry.

Readers of Theocritus will recall how his shepherds contend in song over the charms of their beloved maidens, in Idyll V and elsewhere. (See Lang's translation, The Macmillan Company, New York, 1889.) A study of the evolution of the debate, or disputation, will prove a good introduction to the world of late classical and of mediæval literature. There are many examples of debate, such as those between "The Heart and the Eye," "The Body and the Soul," "The Water and the Wine," "The Owl and the Nightingale," "The Thrush and the Nightingale," "The Debate of the Carpenter's Tools," "The Dispute between Mary and the Cross," and many others. Birds, flowers, animals, inanimate objects, human beings, and even virtuous abstractions were turned into mediæval disputants.

For information regarding debates, and for bibliographies of edited debates, see

MERRILL, E. The Dialogue in English Literature. Henry Holt and Company, New York, 1911.

WELLS, J. E., Editor. The Owl and the Nightingale, p. liii. D. C. Heath & Co., Boston, 1907.

SCHOFIELD, W. H. English Literature from the Norman Conquest to Chaucer, p. 485. The Macmillan Company, New York, 1906.

THE PLEADING OF THE ROSE AND OF THE VIOLET

Jean Froissart (1338-1410) was a distinguished French author who is best known for the famous "Chronicles of England, France, and Spain," which picture with extraordinary vividness scenes which Froissart actually witnessed.

In 1392, probably, Froissart wrote his "Plaidorie de la Rose et de la Violette," which is here translated from his "Poésies," edited in three volumes, with an excellent introduction, by A. Scheler, Brussels, 1872. The value of his poetical works lies in their revelation of the literary taste of the court and of the fashionable world of the day, for he employed the artificial sentiment and the conventional forms of dream and allegory very pleasantly. The Plaidorie is not a famous poem, but it is chosen because it serves to illustrate a combination of various important traits. It is one of the many mediæval poems in which the flower *motif* is preëminent. Here Froissart introduces rather charming personifications, especially significant in the case of the fleur-de-lys, the national flower of France. In spite of the trivial and sentimental attitude towards nature there are many passages of genuine feeling. The poem should be compared with Chaucer's "Prologue to the Legend of Good Women," where the cult of the daisy is represented. Valuable aids to this study will be found in the following articles:

LOWES, J. L. The Prologue to the Legend of Good Women as related to the French Marguerite Poems. *Publications of the Modern Language Association,* XIX, 593-683.

MARSH, G. P. The Sources of the Flower and the Leaf. *Modern Philology,* IV, 121-167, 281-327.

Furthermore, the jesting mockery of legal procedure should be noted. Chaucer's "Fortune" employs legal phraseology, and although Froissart's poem may never have been known to Chaucer, the use of the terms and the associations of law was frequent among poets. Readers of Shakespeare's "Sonnets" will recall his use of legal imagery, but of course he was uninfluenced by this poem.

VISION

THE PURGATORY OF SAINT PATRICK

This translation is a free rendering of a poem found in the famous Auchinleck manuscript, a collection of popular poetry copied in the fourteenth century. A description of this manuscript will be found in Scott's edition of "Sir Tristem." The poem is in the six-line, tail-rime stanza which was much used in romances of the day. There are other versions of this legend in Latin, in French, and in English. Because of its detail, this version, of the late thirteenth century, edited by E. Koelbing in *Englische Studien,* I, 98, has been chosen, although in some respects it is inferior in style to the other English versions. Especially interesting is the picture of the earthly paradise, which is nowhere else described so fully as it is here by catalogues and other means. As an introduction to mediæval religious beliefs the poem is almost unequaled. Pilgrimages, even to this day, are made, by the faithful, to Lough Derg, in Ireland, where Saint Patrick's Purgatory is still continuing its saving grace.

Students of comparative literature recognize in the story a body of tradition reaching back into remote times and forward to the Renaissance, finding its most perfect expression in Dante's "Divine Comedy" (1321). Mediæval descriptions of hell and heaven were made more vivid by adopting the literary form known as the *vision*. The most familiar sort of vision is that which describes things seen in a dream, after the author has fallen asleep. "The Pilgrim's Progress" is an example of this type. Another sort of vision is that which relates what has been perceived by some one in a state of mystical exaltation, as in the Apocalypse of Saint John. The most realistic form of vision is that of "Saint Patrick's Purgatory," where the experiences are described as if actually undergone, and yet they so transcend human probability that the reader recognizes the apocalyptic element. The term "vision" is usually applied to poems describing mysteries of religious or moral truth, and "dream" is applied to secular works such as "The Romance of the Rose," and many other popular poems. Examples of visions from various epochs should be read in order to trace the history. Easily accessible texts in translation are

ST. JOHN. Revelation. (King James Version.)

HOMER. Odyssey, Book XI (translated by G. H. Palmer). Houghton Mifflin Company, Boston, 1891.

VIRGIL. Æneid, Book VI (translated by J. Conington). The Macmillan Company, New York, 1910.

CICERO. Scipio's Dream (translated by C. R. Edmonds in the Bohn Library Cicero). The Macmillan Company, New York.

BEDE. The Vision of Dryhthelm (in Cook and Tinker's "Old English Prose," p. 58). Ginn and Company, Boston, 1908.

DANTE. The Divine Comedy (translated by C. E. Norton). Houghton Mifflin Company, Boston, 1893.

The Pearl (translated by S. Jewett). Thomas Y. Crowell Company, New York, 1908.

For critical studies of the vision and for exhaustive bibliographies of the subject, see

Apocalypse. Encyclopædia Britannica.

WRIGHT, T. Saint Patrick's Purgatory. London, 1844.

KRAPP, G. P. The Legend of Saint Patrick's Purgatory. John Murphy Company, Baltimore, 1900.

BECKER, E. Mediæval Visions of Heaven and Hell. John Murphy Company, Baltimore, 1899.

LANGLOIS, E. Origines et sources du Roman de la Rose, chap. v. Paris, 1890.

For information regarding the dream *motif* in mediæval poems, see

OWEN, D. Piers Plowman, A Comparison with some Earlier and Contemporary French Allegories, pp. 134-167. Hodder and Stoughton, London, 1912.

NEILSON, W. A. The Origins and Sources of the Court of Love. (See "Dream-setting" in the index.) Ginn and Company, Boston, 1899.

Accounts of purgatory and of the terrestrial paradise will be found in "The Catholic Encyclopaedia." Further details regarding the earthly paradise are in Genesis ii, 8-17; Ezekiel xxviii, 13; "Phœnix," in Cook and Tinker's "Old English Poetry"; "Mandeville's Travels," XXXIII, and in Milton's "Paradise Lost," IV. Two critical studies of importance are

GOULD, S. B. Curious Myths of the Middle Ages. London, 1874.

COLI, E. Il Paradiso Terrestre. Florence, 1897

SAINTS' LIVES

THE LIFE OF SAINT BRANDON

Brandon, Brendon, or Brandan, was an Irish Odysseus whose journeyings in search of the Land of Behest have a lasting fascination for all lovers of romantic adventure. The atmosphere of sanctity which made this legend approved reading for the mediæval Christian gives a quaint irony to the accounts of fairies, demons, enchanted birds, and other marvels which betray a frankly superstitious spirit. Travelers' records have a distinct place in literature, as the names Ohthere, Marco Polo, Mandeville, Hakluyt, Robinson Crusoe, Stevenson, Hearn and many others prove, and when the voyage is undertaken because of mingled love of excitement, passion for the sea, zeal for discovery, and deep longing to find the ideal land, it has potent appeal to those who stay at home. In almost every language there are tales which picture an earthly paradise. The Fortunate Isles, the Garden of the Hesperides, Calypso's Isle, Avalon, Hy Brasail, Tir-na'n-Og, are names given in Greek and in Celtic story to the abode of those who have won release from earthly cares and hardship, and have entered the realm of perfect terrestrial peace and beauty.

The translation is William Caxton's version of the life of Brandon based upon some source not yet satisfactorily determined. Caxton's rather rambling but most charming rendering was included in "The Golden Legend," mentioned below.

An exhaustive study of the Irish story upon which this legend is based, and much other material relating to this theme, will be found in Meyer and Nutt's "The Voyage of Bran. Edited and translated by K. Meyer. With an Essay upon the Irish Version of the Happy Other-world and the Celtic Doctrine of Rebirth, by A. Nutt." 2 vols., David Nutt, London, 1895. Interesting also in connection with Brandon is the story of Sindbad, in "The Arabian Nights."

THE LIFE OF SAINT MARGARET

Jacobus de Voragine (1230-1298), Archbishop of Genoa, was the author of "Historia Lombardica seu Legenda Sanctorum," popularly known as "Legenda Aurea." When William Caxton set up his printing press and began to multiply copies of the English classics, he included among his publications an English rendering of the Latin text, "The Golden Legend," (1483), which he based upon a French translation. The present version is from Caxton's text, as printed in the Temple Classics.

The great popularity of lives of the saints is due partly to that trait, inherent in human nature, of genuine devotion to any one of proved courage, especially when that courage is of the spirit, an invincible religious faith and fortitude. Weak and unstable Christians found inspiration in these saintly lives, and by continued meditation learned many lessons of deep meaning. But, in addition to the ethical interest, there was sympathy for the human experiences and the strange and fearful adventures of these elect of the Lord. As the metrical romances ministered to popular delight in knightly deeds, so, too, these legends of the saints satisfied the world-old love of struggle and of victory. Saint Margaret, Saint Katherine, Saint Juliana, were the women saints whose lives were best known to the Middle Ages, but the many legendaries of the day gave ample record of scores of other saints.

For versions of the life of Saint Margaret, see Early English Text Society, No. 13. "The Golden Legend" in seven volumes (Temple Classics, E. P. Dutton and Company, New York) contains the fullest collection of lives of the saints. Middle English collections have been edited by Carl Horstmann. Fox's "Book of Martyrs" should be remembered, also.

PIOUS TALES

The superstitions of the Middle Ages reveal themselves very fully in the various accounts of miracles performed by God, Christ, the Virgin, the saints, or by the relics treasured in churches and religious houses. The study of mediæval religious life must include an examination of some of these fervent and naïve records of the supernatural power of holy objects and holy folk. The intense reverence accorded to sanctified things created, among mediæval Christians, a passionate disregard for the dictates of human reason. At first this blind faith and total abasement before sacred relics was a triumph of the spirit, but before long it became a triumph of the body, for physical well-being and material prosperity were sought rather than spiritual enlightenment. In Chaucer's Pardoner's "Prologue" and in Erasmus's account of his journeys to Walsingham and to Canterbury one finds pictured the credulous and wholly unlovely side of the subject. When idealism declines and becomes sheer bigotry, without the charm of imaginative power, it must have its Wiclif and its Luther.

A MIRACLE OF GOD'S BODY

"A Miracle of God's Body" is translated from Robert Mannyng of Brunne's "Handlyng Synne" (Manual of Sins). Early English Text Society, No. 123, p. 333. See also p. 172 under Homily.

A MIRACLE OF THE VIRGIN

"A Miracle of the Virgin" is from a group of eight miracles, printed in Horstmann's edition of "The Minor Poems of the Vernon Manuscript." Early English Text Society, Part I, No. 98, pp. 138-166.

Other legends connected with the Virgin are to be found in the following volumes:

UNDERHILL, E. The Miracles of Our Lady. E. P. Dutton & Company, New York, 1906.

VINCENT, E. The Madonna of Legend and History. T. Whittaker, New York, 1899.

KEMP WELCH, A., Translator. The Miracles of Our Lady, by Gautier de Coincy. Duffield & Company, New York, 1911.

THE TRANSLATION OF SAINT THOMAS OF CANTERBURY

"The Translation of Saint Thomas of Canterbury" comes from Caxton's "Golden Legend," which should be consulted for a long account of the life of Thomas. Dean Stanley's "Memorials of Canterbury," now published in Everyman's Library, is an indispensable volume for the student.

ALLEGORY

The popularity of allegory, in the Middle Ages, as a means of conveying religious and moral truth, led to the production of many very complex narratives and sermons. An acquaintance with "Piers Plowman" will reveal the character of these works where the reader is soon lost in the labyrinth of abstract names. "The Romance of the Rose," translated by F. S. Ellis (Temple Classics, 3 vols., E. P. Dutton & Company, New York), is the most important example of secular allegory in the Middle Ages. "The Order of Chivalry," a poem that defines the symbolism of the knightly habit, will be found in Miss Butler's "Tales from the Old French," Houghton Mifflin Company, Boston, 1910, and also (as "Sir Hugh of Tabarie") in E. Mason's "Aucassin and Nicolette and Other Mediæval Romances" (Everyman's Library, E. P. Dutton & Company, New York, 1909).

For discussion of the origin and development of mediæval allegory, the reader should consult

NEILSON, W. A. Origins and Sources of the Court of Love. See "Allegory" in the index. Ginn and Company, Boston, 1899.

LANGLOIS, E. Origines et sources du Roman de la Rose, chap. iv. Paris, 1890.

OWEN, D. Piers Plowman, A Comparison with French Allegories. Hodder and Stoughton, London, 1912.

"THE CASTLE OF LOVE"

This extract from a long and very complex poem illustrates significant aspects of mediæval religious allegory. The poem itself was written in French by Robert Grosseteste, Bishop of Lincoln (who died in 1253), and was translated into English several times because of its great popularity. Beginning with an account of the Creation and of the Fall of Man, the poet went on to tell a parable of a Being who had one Son, His equal in all ways, four daughters (named Mercy, Truth, Right, and Peace), and a thrall (named Adam), who was in prison. Mercy and Peace pleaded for the thrall's releases, but Truth and Right objected, so the thrall was punished. Mercy and Peace fled from the land, and the world (except Noah and his family) was drowned. Peace once more appealed for the ransom of the thrall, and the King's Son, hearing the dispute of the four sisters, said He would put on the garments of the thrall and force Peace and Right to be reconciled, and the world would be saved. So Christ entered into the Castle of Love, and was born on earth for the redemption of mankind. An account of the life and passion and resurrection of Christ is given, and the poem concludes with a prayer that we may all be led by Him to everlasting bliss.

The best edition of the English version is

HORSTMANN, C. "The Minor Poems of the Vernon Manuscript," Part I, Early English Text Society, No. 98. This edition contains a version made in the latter part of the thirteenth century, and also a version by a monk of Sawley, in Yorkshire. The present extract is taken from the Sawley monk's translation (ll. 361-452) because that version gives the allegory in more coherent and careful detail than do the other versions, which fail to explain some of the symbolism.

BESTIARY

LION, EAGLE, WHALE, SIREN

From earliest times animals have been employed as symbolic figures by teachers and preachers, and the interest of the present day in animal life and lore is evidence of the never-failing pleasure humanity finds in beast books. Æsop's "Fables," "The Little Flowers of Saint Francis," "Reynard the Fox," and "The Jungle Stories" illustrate various sides of the literature about the lesser folk. The mediæval bestiary was a book which sought to enunciate religious instruction by an appeal to the curiosity of credulous people. The didactic interest far exceeded the scientific in these allegories which, to us, are most diverting matter. The source of the bestiary is to be found in the Greek "Physiologus" (second century A.D.), which was translated into Latin by Theobaldus in the late Middle Ages, and then into other languages. In Old English literature "The Whale" and "The Panther" and a fragment of "The Partridge" are all that remain of the version in that language. The Middle English bestiary of the thirteenth century contains descriptions, followed by explication, of the lion, the eagle, the adder, the ant, the hart, the fox, the spider, the whale, the siren, the elephant, the turtle dove, the panther, and the culver. There is a French bestiary written in England by Philippe de Thaün, about 1120, which contains a portion of a lapidary also. A translation is in T. Wright's "Popular Treatises on Science written during the Middle Ages." London, 1841.

The text of the Middle English bestiary may be found in

MORRIS, R. An Old English Miscellany. Early English Text Society, No. 49.

MAETZNER, E. Altenglische Sprachproben, I, 55. Berlin, 1867.

WRIGHT, T., and HALLIWELL, J. O. Reliquiae Antiquae, I, 208. London, 1845.

Suggestive studies on the subject are

KITTREDGE, G. L. Beast Fables, in Johnson's Universal Cyclopædia.

LAND, J. P. N. Physiologos, in Encyclopædia Britannica.

LAUCHERT, F. Geschichte des Physiologus. Strassburg, 1889.

In the popular mediæval epic, "Reynard the Fox," animals, very realistically portrayed, yet with satirical symbolism, are the actors in a story full of interest to the modern reader. This is accessible in the following English versions:

CAXTON, W. Reynard the Fox. Percy Society, Vol. XII. London.

MORLEY, H. Early English Prose Romances. E. P. Dutton and Company, New York, 1912.

JACOBS, J. The Most Delectable History of Reynard the Fox. Macmillan and Company, London, 1895.

LAPIDARY

SELECTIONS FROM LAPIDARIES

Marbodus, Bishop of Rennes in the twelfth century, was the author of the lapidary which was best known during the Middle Ages. This book, called "De Gemmis," was written in Latin verse, and gives the strange superstitions about the virtues and efficacies of sixty stones. Many of these stones are now unknown to us. There was so much interest in this lapidary that it was frequently translated into French, both in verse form and in prose, and was popular in England as well as in France. The traditions about stones developed two sorts of treatise: one in which the purely pagan beliefs are represented, as they were handed down by Aristotle, Pliny, Marbodus, and others; and a second in which the pagan superstitions are inwrought with Christian teachings and associated with Scriptural passages. In translating Marbodus, a Christian clerk would add and alter material in such a way as to impress religious symbolisms upon his readers, through the popular interest in all the lore of stones.

Information regarding the lapidaries, as well as editions of various French and other lapidaries, will be found in the following books:

PANNIER, L. Les Lapidaires français du moyen-âge des XIIe, XIIIe, et XIVe siècles. Paris, 1882.

MEYER, P. Les Plus Anciens Lapidaires français. *Romania* (Jan., Avril, Oct.). Paris, 1909.

KING, C. W. Antique Gems. Contains a translation of the work of Marbodus. London, 1860.

STREETER, E. W. Precious Stones and Gems, their History, Sources, and Characteristics. Illustrated in color. London, 1898.

WRIGHT, T. Popular Treatises on Science written during the Middle Ages. London, 1841.

The accounts of diamond, sapphire, amethyst, geratite, chelidonius, coral, heliotrope, pearl, and pantheros are translated from a French prose version of the Latin of Marbodus. The French translation was made, perhaps, in England during the twelfth century. The text will be found in Meyer, pp. 271-285. The French prose lapidary has been chosen rather than that in verse form, because it has fewer tags and circumlocutions, and can be more faithfully rendered into English.

The diamond, or adamant, was a favorite stone. "The Travels of Sir John Mandeville," pp. 105-108, The Macmillan Company, New York, 1905, has an interesting account of this.

The pearl has been the subject of much discussion. The present translation omits several lines in the French version which do not appear in Marbodus and which seem to be due to confusion with another stone. Consult Kunz and Stevenson's "The Book of the Pearl," The Century Company, New York, 1908, and pp. 599-610 of Schofield's article "Symbolism, Allegory, and Autobiography in The Pearl." *Publications of the Modern Language Association*, Vol. XVII.

The extract describing the carbuncle is from Pannier, p. 295, where a prose fragment of a Christian lapidary is given. The carbuncle was frequently mentioned in mediæval romances, and was supposed to give success in battle, and also in lawsuits (see Meyer, p. 67).

The account of the symbolism of the twelve stones comes from Philippe de Thaün's "Bestiaire," verses 2977-3004. The Oxford Bible gives classified lists of stones mentioned in the Scriptures.

HOMILY

CONCERNING MIRACLE PLAYS, GAMES, AND MINSTRELSY

Homilies in prose and in verse were a common means of instruction. They were usually more popular than mere sermons and sought to hold the attention by the use of copious illustration. The following extract is from "Handlyng Synne" (Manual of Sins), translated in 1303 by Robert Mannyng of Brunne, from a French original, and edited by Dr. Furnivall, Early English Text Society, No. 119. "Handlyng Synne," a collection of homilies, denounces the seven deadly sins, citing many concrete instances of fact and of fable in order to enforce the moral lessons. The translation below interprets lines 4637-4774 (pp. 155-159), where the sin of sloth is under discussion.

For information about minstrelsy the student should consult

CHAMBERS, E. K. The Mediæval Stage, Vol. I, bk. i. Oxford University Press, 1903.

GALPIN, F. W. Old English Instruments of Music. A. C. McClurg & Co., Chicago, 1911.

DUNCAN, E. The Story of Minstrelsy. Charles Scribner's Sons, New York, 1907.

CUTTS, E. Scenes and Characters of the Middle Ages. Vertue and Company, London, 1886.

SATIRE

The most popular satire in the Middle Ages is found in the fabliaux, short tales which picture, with great zest, racy incidents in the lives of common people whose hidden sins or hypocrisies are suddenly exposed. The satire in these stories is exceedingly broad and attacks, by preference, women and the clergy, painting with vivid realism their immorality and intense selfishness. Readers will find information regarding these in "The English Fabliau," by H. S. Canby, *Publications of the Modern Language Association*, XXI, 200-214. Formal satire, which points out abuses and vices by means of exposition, is illustrated in the poems following. Satire against women is most agreeably found in "The Romance of the Rose," chaps. xlvi-lii (translated by F. S. Ellis, Temple Classics). In *Romania*, XV, 315, 339; XVI, 389; XXXVI, 1, will be found interesting matter relating to satires on women, in France.

THE SONG OF THE UNIVERSITY OF PARIS

This is freely translated from the French poem of Rutebeuf, written in octosyllabic couplets, about the middle of the thirteenth century. Rutebeuf was a famous minstrel whose vivid wit gave him a distinguished place among mediæval writers. His works are full of autobiographical details; he pictured his unhappy domestic life, his poverty, all his failings, and his virtues with an engaging frankness. In allegory he was a master of the mannerisms of his day. In satire he was original and clever. The monastic orders aroused his fiercest resentment, and he made sharp epigrams at their expense, accusing them of committing the seven deadly sins and more. The dry incisiveness of his ridicule may have impressed Chaucer and also the author of "Piers Plowman," although we have no proof of this. A very good study of Rutebeuf has been published by L. Cledat, Paris, 1891. The description of the mediæval student gives a true picture of the day, but Chaucer's description of the Clerk of Oxford should be read as complement. For details regarding student life of the Middle Ages, consult

RASHDALL, H. The Universities of Europe in the Middle Ages, 3 vols. London, 1895.

HEWETT, W. T. University Life in the Middle Ages. *Harper's Magazine*, 1897.

SYMONDS, J. A. Wine, Women and Song (translations of many student songs of the Middle Ages). Chatto and Windus, London, 1907.

THE LAND OF COCKAYGNE

The meaning of *Cockaygne* is usually understood to be "cookery." This satire upon the mediæval monks was probably derived from a French original. It illustrates the contemptuous tolerance of that day for the greed, the gluttony, the slothfulness, and the immorality of the inmates of the monastery. The satire directed against literary conventions of the day is particularly amusing, if we notice how the various catalogues of animals, birds, spices, flowers, jewels, and food parody similar catalogues in the romances and in the poems describing paradise. The poem was written, in the short couplet, about the middle of the thirteenth century. It is printed in E. Maetzner's "Altenglische Sprachproben," I, 148. Berlin, 1867. Wright's "St. Patrick's Purgatory," London, 1844, contains an interesting chapter on this and similar burlesques.

THE COMPLAINT OF THE HUSBANDMAN

This "complaint," or "song," was written during the thirteenth century when the persecutions of the poor farmers by lords and their officers were most extreme. The poem explains very fully the various abuses which finally so incensed the poor that they rose in revolt and won certain rights from their oppressors. The Middle English text is found in K. Boeddeker's "Altenglische Dichtungen," p. 102, Berlin, 1878, and in T. Wright's "Political Songs," Camden Society, Vol. VI, p. 149.

The meter and rime of the original have been kept, in this translation, even at the risk of a few very slight changes in the order or in the phrasing of the original, because the versification is so illustrative of the transition from the old alliterative line to the elaborate stanza forms of the French period.

SIR PENNY

This satire was evidently a popular one in the Middle Ages; it is found in various forms in Latin, in French, and in English. The following translation is made from a version, probably of about 1350, printed in Thomas Wright's "Latin Poems attributed to Walter Mapes," Camden Society, Vol. XVI, pp. 359-361. The poem is written in the six-line, tail-rime stanza of "Sir Thopas," and the translation seeks to preserve the cadences, movement, and structure of the original. It is interesting in connection with "Piers Plowman" and "The Pardoner's Tale," for it shows the great superiority of those satires, in imaginative appeal. The generalizations here are faithful, but they lack point and effectiveness because they do not drive home specific instances about individuals. We have a personal interest in Lady Meed and in the Pardoner, but we care little about classes and types.

LAY

SIR ORFEO

This Middle English version of a French lay seems to offer so few difficulties that it is given in its original form, as it appears in the Auchinleck manuscript. The text is copied from that edited by Laing in "Select Pieces of Ancient Popular Poetry of Scotland," reprinted in Edinburgh, 1884. A critical edition of the poem was published by O. Zielke, Breslau, 1880. A very charming free translation in stanza form has been made by E. E. Hunt, Cambridge, 1909.

"Sir Orfeo" is the mediæval interpretation of the story of Orpheus and Eurydice (Ovid's "Metamorphoses," bk. x, ll. 1-77), which was told in French, and then translated by some nameless but immortal English poet. The beauty of this Middle English version is undeniable. Despite its brevity and its occasionally laconic phrases, the poem shows real pathos in the account of the passionate grief of Orfeo, and his desolate wanderings in search of his lady. The concrete vividness of color and fragrance in nature, the dim stateliness of the retinue of the king of fairyland, the magic beauty of his strange abode, are described with true poetic sensitiveness. In choice of detail, in management of incident, in "discovery," and in conclusion the narrative is singularly well managed.

As a mediæval rendering of a classical tale, the poem has many charms, because it so naïvely and so completely changes the setting and insists upon mediæval towers and dress and customs. Pluto's dark realm is transformed into a fairy kingdom, Thrace has become Winchester, and the wandering

Greek is a Breton harper knocking at the door of a Gothic castle. As a version of one of the most beautiful of the world's stories, this lay has true imaginative distinction; it pictures the loyalty of love and love's power over time and fairy spells, but it willfully changes the outcome of the old story to suit the sentiment of high romance in an age when every tale must have a happy ending.

Other lays, or brief tales, are described in W. H. Schofield's "English Literature from the Norman Conquest to Chaucer," p. 179. The Macmillan Company, New York, 1906. "Launfal," a lay of fairyland, is one of the most beautiful. The lays of Marie de France are accessible in the following translations:

WESTON, J. Four Lais of Marie de France (including "Launfal"). Charles Scribner's Sons, New York, 1901.

RICKERT, E. Seven Lais of Marie de France. Charles Scribner's Sons, New York, 1901.

Fairy lore is discussed by many students. The volumes named below will be found serviceable to the student of English literature:

PATON, L. A. Studies in the Fairy Mythology of Arthurian Romance. Ginn and Company, Boston, 1903.

NUTT, A. The Fairy Mythology of Shakespeare. David Nutt, London, 1900.

HAZLITT, W. C. Fairy Tales, Lays, and Romances Illustrating Shakespeare. London, 1875.

SIDGWICK, F. The Sources and Analogues of "A Midsummer Night's Dream." Duffield & Company, New York, 1908.

In translating the poem the student should pronounce all the unknown words aloud and he will speedily recognize resemblances to modern words. Y is the pronoun "I," but sometimes it is part of the past participle,—*y-hold* = "held." *Ich* is "I," and also "each." Frequently a pronoun and a verb are combined, as *ichil* = "I will"; *wiltow* = "wilt thou"; sometimes the negative particle is combined with a verb, as in *nis* = "is not"; *nil* = "will not." *Owhen* = "own"; *yif* = "if." It is assumed that readers will recognize the words used in the ballads or in Spenser's works. If there are words which are not recognized they can be found in the New English Dictionary, or in the New International Dictionary, or in Bradley and Stratmann's Middle English Dictionary.

FOOTNOTES:

[1] Temple Classics, 3 vols. Dutton, New York, 1900.

[2] B. Smythe, Trobador Poets. (Translations.) Duffield, New York, 1911.

[3] See Notes.

[4] See Notes.

[5] varied.

[6] equal.

[7] disagreement.

[8] love.

[9] pleasure.

[10] describe.

[11] equal.

[12] quickness.

[13] breastplate.

[14] comprehend.

[15] Achilles.

[16] together.

[17] see.

[18] interval of a fifth.

[19] nightingale.

[20] music.

[21] color.

[22] staggers.

[23] in fief.

[24] love.

[25] See Notes.

[26] See Notes.

[27] Fifteen, in other versions.

[28] Other versions say that the bridge grew wider and wider as Owain passed over it.

[29] A stringed instrument.

[30] Here is a gap of two stanzas and more, pursuing the theme of Adam.

[31] See Notes.

[32] scarcely.

[33] refectory.

[34] ordinary.

[35] hermits.

[36] Thursday before Easter.

[37] griffin.

[38] with hair.

[39] See Notes.

[40] See Notes.

[41] See Notes.

[42] See Notes.

[43] See Notes.

[44] The four cardinal virtues: Fortitude, Temperance, Justice, and Prudence.

[45] See Notes.

[46] See Notes.

[47] See Notes.

[48] See Notes.

[49] See Notes.

[50] According to G. Paris he played on cymbals and exhibited a monkey.

[51] See Notes.

[52] See Notes.

[53] See Notes.

[54] hedge-warden, over-seer.

[55] under-steward.

[56] wood-warden.

[57] religious orders.

[58] peasant.

[59] over-seers.

[60] wax for king's seal.

[61] salmon.

[62] implement for pruning.

[63] See Notes.

[64] See Notes.

[65] both.

[66] called.

[67] lady.

[68] time.

[69] bright, vigorous.

[70] same.

[71] forenoon.

[72] grafted.

[73] rubbed, wrung.

[74] rent.

[75] removed.

[76] ran.

[77] away.

[78] took.

[79] dear.

[80] thee.

[81] criest.

[82] shrill.

[83] before.

[84] complexion.
[85] eyes.
[86] very.
[87] since.
[88] must.
[89] directly.
[90] again.
[91] forest.
[92] places.
[93] taken.
[94] woe.
[95] lose.
[96] defence.
[97] taken.
[98] dole.
[99] order.
[100] lost.
[101] roam.
[102] woods.
[103] scarcely.
[104] together.
[105] pilgrim's robe.
[106] however.
[107] ease.
[108] discomfort.
[109] fur (variegated).
[110] fur (gray).
[111] linen.
[112] wraps.

[113] moss (?).

[114] grub.

[115] shrunken.

[116] rough.

[117] gather.

[118] at last.

[119] about.

[120] branch.

[121] accustomed.

[122] speedily (?).

[123] royal.

[124] grandly.

[125] front.

[126] adorned.

[127] dwellings.

[128] dark (?).

[129] sapphires are mentioned in one version.

[130] lying.

[131] head.

[132] had no arms.

[133] mad.

[134] drowned.

[135] withered.

[136] mad (?).

[137] sport.

[138] ceased.

[139] hue.

[140] therefore.

[141] lie.

[142] just now.

[143] warmly.

[144] quickly.

[145] people, land.

[146] went.

[147] harbor.

[148] cottage.

[149] bit.

[150] back.

[151] withered.

[152] players on the *crowd*, a kind of violin.

[153] ate.

[154] lost.

[155] given.

[156] hour.

[157] remedy.

[158] gracious.

[159] inn.

[160] awe.

[161] understood.

[162] table.

[163] quickly.

[164] indeed.

[165] named.

[166] called.